THE

WEB TRAFFIC

BOOK

A Definitive Guide To Crushing Your Competitors And Getting All The Customers You Ever Need.

ROSS GOLDBERG

Author Ross Goldberg

The Web Traffic Book

A Definitive Guide To Crushing Your Competitors And Getting All The Customers You Ever Need.

Disclaimer

Credits

Special thanks to

Alan Bechtold, David Bullock, Corena Golliver, Sohail Kahn, Anik Singal, Mari Smith, Erik Stafford, & Vin Montello

TABLE OF CONTENTS

4

This book is dedicated to all the people that have helped me along the way...

Harris Fellman: My sounding board and closest advisor.

Erik Stafford: My partner and brother from another mother.

My Taylor, Breanna, and Shawn: I live for you.

My Jaime: The amazing woman that is just crazy enough to put up with my crap and always says "OK baby, do your thing".

INTRODUCTION: BY ERIC STAFFORD

It happened over soup.

Vietnamese soup, actually...

You see, Ross and I live in the same, sleepy town here in South Florida.

We tend to get together once or twice a week, to work on our laptops in the coffee shop, or have lunch, or just to talk about marketing. We share strategies, plot together, and have helped each other in countless ways over the years.

Anyways, when Ross told me he was writing a book, he told me over soup.

He said it would be THE definitive book on Web Traffic – A book containing every single thing he learned over the years about how to get the right visitors to your website pages.

I told him I thought it was a great idea.

In my opinion, there isn't a person alive who is more qualified to write a comprehensive book on Web Traffic, and I him told that, as well.

I only had one question.

What about the people who don't yet have a website?

After all, what use is it to drive visitors to a website... If you don't have one?

Ross kinda gave me one of those looks, as if to say, "You're the website guy... Figure something out!"

So, I promised him that day that if he ever did indeed write THE definitive book on Website Traffic, I would go out of my way to help those people who weren't even at square one yet.

As you probably guessed by now, the book, he mentioned to me that day was in fact THIS book, the one you are reading at this moment.

And it's worth its weight in GOLD.

I plan to recommend this book to every single one of the people I work with each and every year...

And I also plan on sticking to the promise I made to Ross that day:

Those of you who don't yet have a website: It's my pleasure to offer you complimentary access to The Faster Webmaster.

The course is ten simple steps to building your first website in the quickest, easiest, and most affordable way possible.

The course contains step-by-step instructions... and videos, so you can follow along and watch everything I do.

"He said it would be THE definitive book on Web Traffic – A book containing every single thing he learned over the years about how to get the right visitors to your website pages..."

You can grab your free account here: www.thefasterwebmaster.com/trafficbook

I hope you enjoy this surprise bonus...

And once you get your website up and running I encourage you to absolutely devour this book: *Write notes in the margins, underline key points, and dog-ear important pages.*

Because Ross's methods work, plain and simple.

Here's to your success!

Erik Stafford,

The Faster Webmaster

www.thefasterwebmaster.com/trafficbook

P.S. - Ross: Great job on the book, man. And thanks for the soup!

> "...Ross's methods work, plain and simple."
>
> ~Eric Stafford

PRELOGUE

My story starts off wonderful, dips into incredible, and turns into almost unbelievable, but we'll save the most of the juicier details for another time.

The short version that leads to the beginning of my journey as an Internet entrepreneur is this:

I'm a retired gang leader and a disabled veteran.

Again, it's a long story...

In July of 2005, I was attending the University of Whitewater in Whitewater, Wisconsin, majoring in Psychology. The Department of Veterans Affairs had covered my tuition and was giving us $1,000 per month to live on. The problem is that I have a wife and 3 kids to care for and it was barely enough to cover our monthly diaper expense at the time.

I turned to my wife one day and said, "Honey, I'm always on the Internet for school and know my way around. I think I'm going to look for a product we can sell online to get us out of this rotten financial mess we're in."

I was barely coping with Fibromyalgia, which left me in a ton of pain (I was on morphine to control it) and I had a huge amount of trouble sleeping. Due to those issues, it was impossible for me to hold a job.

Her response was; "OK baby, do your thing".

So, I dove into Internet business and two weeks later we had products up for sale on Ebay® (no, this isn't a "how-to" sell the stuff, you don't want, on Ebay book).

Two weeks after that, my body stopped working and I went into a coma.

I was comatose for 10 days and my version of the movie Fight Club© played out in my head. Either I, or those I heard or saw in my hospital room, would be fighting strange, monstrous "guys" that looked like they had been built for pure destruction. If I wasn't fighting these monsters, I was coaching somebody else who was.

I woke from the coma 10 days later with pneumonia and no feeling from my waist down.

I regained enough feeling in my legs to move them, but still have nerve damage that prevents me from feeling temperature and anything else other than pain from my chest to my toes.

I spent 3 weeks in major rehabilitation to regain my ability to function and walk. During that time, my wife and brother had figured out how to fulfill orders for our fresh, new business.

I went home wheelchair-bound and was surprised to find $1,000 profit in our PayPal® account.

That was all I needed to see and was immediately motivated to figure out the ins and outs of making money online.

I quickly realized that Ebay was taking 10% of profit between Ebay and PayPal fees and had the bright idea of putting a website together. My family had been poor for so long and was finally making some money, so I spent 2 hours per day fulfilling orders and creating new Ebay listings and the other 12 hours per day that I worked was devoted to learning everything I could about web design.

Once I'd gotten our hideous website done, I put it up and breathed a long sigh of relief. I fully expected sales to start pouring in.

They didn't.

In fact, it took Google™ 60 days to find the website at all. Then, they listed it on page 114 for any of our chosen keywords that I wanted to rank for.

The next step was to figure out how to fix our rotten search engine rankings. Another few hundred hours later and my site was on page 2 for our main keywords. It wasn't easy, but after a ton of really bad ideas I found some that actually worked (including some that most people hadn't even considered or discovered yet).

On the one year anniversary of this business, I had done just under half a million dollars in sales and had to shut it down. A vendor had robbed us of $5,000 and we had spent every nickel of profit that had come in.

After a short stint doing SEO (search engine optimization) for other companies, I wrote my first digital book (or Ebook) that taught others how to get their websites to rank in the search engines.

Since that first book, I have made some simple accomplishments:

- I put on six Internet marketing seminars (four live and two virtual).
- I've released over a dozen Internet marketing training products.
- Launched 3 different traffic generating software programs.
- I worked as Vice President of Marketing for StomperNet™ (one of the largest Internet marketing training companies in the world).
- Most importantly, I've helped thousands of people finally get the traffic they need for their websites.
- I've done well over 2 million dollars in sales in less than 5 years online.

<u>By myself.</u>

With <u>no</u> staff…

I'd have to be a certified fool to suggest that you follow my path.

I need to be sure that you know that you can do this before we start this journey. If I can pull off what I've accomplished, I know that you can make this work for you, too.

I spent thousands of dollars and more hours than I care to count on miscellaneous books and software packages that promised to be the "magic bullet" when it comes to getting traffic.

In a short period of time, through a ton of testing and bad ideas, I figured out how the search engines really operate. Before I knew it, my website was in the top 20 for my major keyword terms.

It took me months to figure out what worked and what didn't work in the "eyes" of the major search engines and far more when it comes to getting people to find your websites. The core goal of this book is to ensure that you don't have to work as hard or study as long as I did.

You'll find this information in this book explained in plain English, in a way that most people should be able to easily understand. Soon, you'll have your own action plan and be working toward the goal of dominating your marketplace online.

CHAPTER 1: HOW THEY FIND YOU

BEGIN HERE

The Search Process

Let's kick this off with an example situation, it'll help make sense of the search process and start you off with the right ideas in your head as you start to plan out your traffic strategy:

Brian is looking for a new Television. He begins his search by typing in "TV" into Google™.

The results that come up include, TV.com™, Tvguide.com™, and Hulu.com™ but none of these sites sells Televisions.

Next, Brian searches for HDTV. The search results are a little bit closer to what he's looking. Google shows him a bunch of HDTV product listings with prices as the third listing. He quickly realizes that his searches aren't specific enough to give him the results he wants as fast as he wants them. Brian is getting frustrated over the amount of time and work required for him to simply find what he's looking for.

Finally, Brian looks for "40" LCD HDTV" and gets the results he needs. The first result is more product listings, the next two results are for TVs being sold on Amazon.com™, which Brian trusts, and he purchases the television listed for sale at Amazon for a competitive price. Brian is thrilled that he's finally completed the purchase sequence and can go back to doing more important things.

The search experience for nearly any user that is looking for something specific normally mirrors what Brian went through. It's an irritating experience that leaves people in a situation where they simply want the solution to their problem and when they find it, the credit cards come out quickly.

Keep this in mind as you discover strategies in this book that will give you the ability to cater directly to the people trying to find stuff for sale on the web.

UNDERSTANDING A SEARCH ENGINE

Have you ever looked at the code of a web page? If not, you must see it as soon as you find a spare moment. The code of a webpage is all that a search engine sees when it looks at a website.

Go to any website, preferably your own. Right click with your mouse and select "view source". This lets you view all of the code of any web page.

Search engines send little software robots called "spiders" out into the Internet to index and find websites. Most of them have many spiders. They have spiders for indexing pages, spiders for images, spiders for ads and many more. These spiders go over your website to the best of their ability and bring the information back to the search engines, so they can decide where your site belongs inside their massive index of the Internet.

Your goal is to make it easier for people to find you through search engines and as many other methods as you can.

KEYWORD RESEARCH

Keyword Research is the most important aspect of owning a website.

You MUST understand what search keywords will drive qualified prospects to your website. Otherwise, you will waste a lot of time spinning your wheels to attract people and will end up reaching the wrong ones, or even worse, nobody at all.

Google offers a keyword research tool, designed to help the users of their Adwords[©] program pick terms to target for their business. While it is made for them, anybody can use this tool free. https://adwords.google.com/select/KeywordToolExternal

All you need to do here is enter your most common keyword. The results that come up to start with will be related to the one you entered into their form. It shows you how many searches there were for each term for the previous month and the Adwords competition for each term. The key to good keyword research is not to choose every highly searched term. It would be great to rank for the term 'chair', but if you sell office chairs, it would be better to focus on the keyword terms that will bring you in qualified customers. You should choose one or two short (2 to 3--word) keyword terms to focus on in your website.

You **MUST** also focus on longer keyword terms (4 to 5 words). Traditionally referred to as the "long tail" of search, these keyword terms will bring you in the most qualified customers to your website. By focusing on extremely focused keyword terms in your search marketing strategy, you will have less difficulty ranking for them and will convert more of the visitors into sales. Find buyer focused terms (if you sell known product names, adding the word "buy" to the phrase you are targeting can get you dramatic increases to your conversion rates from prospect to sale).

I always look specifically at the Adwords competition for a term. A green bar shows this in the third column of the keyword research tool. If the green bar is completely full it shows, that the keyword term is very competitive and should be difficult to rank well. If the bar is empty, that tells us that the term either has a very low search volume or is not profitable. The sweet spot is when the bar is between half-full and almost completely full. *Those "middle area" terms are what you should try to find.*

We already went over what an Internet user does when they search for something. Remember that people are more likely to purchase as the search progression moves forward.

"Focus on the long tail terms to convert more customers into buyers."

The key to optimizing your website is to make sure you have optimized for all of the keyword possibilities, as your prospect searches for what you sell. You will be able to rank easiest for the longer terms and should be able to bring the likeliest customer to buy first.

Branded terms are normally quite competitive, but with a little time and some perseverance, you will be able to rank for those terms.

The generic keyword terms are hardest to rank for but with enough blood, sweat, and tears it can be accomplished.

Focus on the long tail terms to convert more customers into buyers.

YOUR WEBSITE ADDRESS

One of the first steps in doing business online is to choose your Uniform Resource Locator (URL) or website address.

The URL is the web address that someone types in when he or she goes to a website. The URL you use for your business is very important and <u>must be chosen carefully</u>. The URL you use must have your most important keywords in the URL whenever possible. If you are offering televisions, you should absolutely have the word "television" in your URL.

The reason you need this is that it is something that you'll get "extra credit" for from the search engines. A domain name can't be changed once it's been purchased. The search engines know this and will rank you for terms in your domain name much faster than if you use other words in it.

Unless your business is already established, you have the ultimate freedom in what your business will be called. If your business already exists, you are more limited as to what URL you choose.

You have specific goals to consider when deciding on a domain name (URL):

1. Is it easy for your customers to remember?

2. Are any of your keywords in it?

3. Does it properly reflect your business?

As you develop (or have developed) your website, make sure you name the pages accordingly. If you have a page dedicated to Phillips® televisions, the pages URL should be Phillips-televisions. Take special care when creating pages to ensure that your keywords are in the URL. Search engines look at individual page URLs and use that as one of the many factors in ranking a page for keywords. Some would recommend Phillipstelevisions, and it works just fine. Every day more domains are sold and most of the best ones are already gone. If you have to, feel free to use hyphens in your domain name.

The most important aspect of your domain name: You must check to see if someone else has ever used your domain.

If your brand new domain name was used for spam or unethical Internet practices, it will be extremely difficult to get it indexed in the major search engines. Believe me, not an issue in which you want to have to deal.

Check out your potential domain name at http://www.archive.org

> *If your brand new domain name was used for spam or unethical Internet practices, it will be extremely difficult to get it indexed in the major search engines.*

Take the time to see if it has ever been pre-owned. If it has been pre-owned, take a look at the archives to see if someone was breaking any rules with this domain (see the next few pages for naughty tricks you should NOT try to use).

You will thank me if you find out that it was abused in the past.

Take my advice and spend two minutes to see if your domain name was ever registered in the past.

CHAPTER 2:THE DARKSIDE OF SEO

Stay away from the dark side of SEO (Search Engine Optimization)

Because of the fierce competition in the SEO industry, some search engine optimization firms began using tactics that the search engines have labeled as "black-hat", or "naughty", in the search engine world.

Every major search engine (Google™, Yahoo®, and Bing™) has issued rules and guidelines listing several of these black-hat tactics. Failure to comply with these guidelines will most likely get you de-indexed, or worse, banned from the search engines. Black hat SEO could be explained as the intentional misleading of search engines and their spiders.

 **Nothing is worth the risk of being permanently booted out of a search engine.**

DO NOT DO ANY OF THESE THINGS TO YOUR WEBSITE!

Keyword Stuffing

Keyword stuffing is the intentional overuse of a particular term or phrase in hopes of achieving higher search engine rankings for that term or phrase. Normally, "stuffing" looks unnatural and will turn away any human being that sees the website.

The best way to avoid this is to fill your page with text written naturally and do not over use your target phrase. Not only is it deceptive, but your customers will see it and run.

Hidden Text

Hidden text is setting the color of text the same as the background of a webpage. By having your text and background the same color, the text or repeating phrases is invisible to human visitors but not search engine bots. Search engines now look for the color of the text and compare it to the color of the background. Some webmasters create a colored image and set it as the background to the page to avoid being detected. Search engines know how to find this and will penalize you heavily when they do.

Cloaking

Cloaking, in short, is intentionally displaying different information to human visitors than to search engines. There are numerous ways of cloaking content, and not all have been determined "black-hat". Black-hat cloaking will work for a short time, however, you run a high risk of having your domain banned permanently. What I'm referring to is purposely misleading the search engines, not things like cloaking an affiliate link (if you don't know what that means, forget that it was mentioned). **There are ethical reasons for cloaking and they are not all bad if used properly.**

Redirects

Redirect pages have several ethical purposes, however, when used as a black-hat tactic – often combined with doorway pages – they serve as a red flag to search engines. Sneaky Redirect pages take a visitor from one page to another automatically and normally are used to guide search engines to page they will like better than the one you send your visitor to.

Duplicate Sites

This is not often used but, when affiliate programs were first gaining in popularity, webmasters would create several copies of the same sales page in hopes that quantity over quality would prevail and they would make a sale from one of their many websites selling a product. With the advancement of search engines, they are able to find excessively duplicate content and will penalize you heavily for it. This is not the fabled "duplicate content penalty", it is just the search engines applying their relevance algorithm (a mathematical equation that search engines use to provide relevant results to their users).

PURCHASING LINKS

The idea behind link building is to have other websites find your website and see the quality it represents. Once that happens, they will link to your website for their customers to utilize. This tactic was very quickly abused as people saw dollar signs and started to link purchasing services.

Purchasing links in bulk with no regard to the site it comes from will give you absolutely no benefit in the eyes of the search engines. In fact, they will penalize your site for having hundreds or thousands of links that point to you for no reason other than you paid them to. The search engines will catch this every time and it will hurt your rankings.

Purchasing links one at a time from related web sites that are similar to your own will give you benefit in rankings.

CHAPTER 3: TAG YOU ARE IT!

META TAGS: THE RIGHT WAY

There are specific "tags" used in the coding of your website that give important information to search engines. These tags are: Title, Keyword, and Description tags.

Here is how you should format your Meta Tags:

<title>Your Company Keyword 1 | Keyword Phrase 2</title>

<META NAME="description" CONTENT="Add 2 to 3 sentences here and be sure to use your main keywords and keyword phrases where you can.">

<META NAME="keywords" CONTENT="Keep this keyword tag simple, only use 5 to 20 keywords and keyword phrases separated by commas">

<META CONTENT="INDEX" NAME="robots">

Replace our company information with the information of your company and place this information between the <head> tags in your page html coding.

The key is to have separate meta tags for each page. This gives you a chance to differentiate each page on your website and improves the ability of the search engines to identify your pages to their users.

Change your Tags for every page to avoid being penalized as a spammer.

Title Tag:

Your title tag is the most important of these tags. Your title tag is what a customer will click on when they find you in the search engine results pages. Include at least one or two of your keyword phrases. Here is the format for a title tag for a site that sells custom blue widgets: "Blue Widgets | Custom Widget Designs". When formatting a title tag, you must use your most important keywords. Notice how I included widget and widgets. This makes sure that search engines recognize that you need to rank for the word and its multiple. You should do this if the searches for widget and widgets are high enough for you to want the traffic from that term. Notice the "|" in between the terms, using the word "and" deters some search engines from looking at the words beyond the phrase "and". In this way, you can use fewer words and have separated the two phrases. In addition, be sure to use the least amount of words possible in the title tag.

You should try to keep your title tag between 40 and 50 characters. Do not ever go over 60 characters. The reasoning for this is that the fewer words you use, the more weight they hold in the eyes of the search engines.

Keyword Tag:

Your keyword tag is not even looked at or considered by some search engines. My recommendation is to keep your keyword tag short and sweet. Use only your most important keywords and their multiples here. I recommend keeping this tag under 100 characters.

The reasoning behind keeping this tag short is that years ago people stuffed so many keywords into this tag that it became abused, which is why search engines don't pay much attention to it today. A keyword tag should be used, but not abused. The less words you use, the more they will mean to the search engines that pay attention to them. Search engines will remove your site from its index if they think you are trying to cheat the system. This is what your keyword tag looks like:

<META NAME="keywords" CONTENT="search engine optimization, search engine placement, seo, optimization services, seo company, search engine optimization firm, diamond seo">

Description Tag:

Your description tag should be made up of a few sentences describing the page that it is on. Normally used as the description search engines use when listing your site in their results, makes it is important to write description tags for your customers and not for the search engines.

Make sure you put a different description tag onto each page.

There should be at least one sentence in every tag. And one sentence on every page that describes that page itself. The reason for this is that as search engines will notice inner pages of your site, they look for indications of pages being different and original. Plus, you want the results to show differently for each page. If you have the same paragraph for every page, a customer may notice and avoid your site. This is another tag that has been abused, so make sure that you keep it simple and don't put in too much information. I recommend 150 to 200 characters in this tag.

This is the way your Description Tag should look:

<META NAME="description" CONTENT="Diamond SEO specializes in organic search engine optimization and web site design to give you permanent high results in search engines.">

There are other tags that you should use in the content of your website. The tags in this section are actually added into your web copy as html code. They will format your text in a manner that shows the search engines that the words (or images) inside of them are important. Normally, they alter the appearance of your web pages, too.

The tags are alt, header, and strong tags.

Alt Tags:

Alt tags are words attach to images that describe what they show someone that sees it on your page. This was initially done so that the blind can hear what they are supposed to see through special software that will "read" the tag for them. Search engines have found that the texts inside these tags are good indicators of what the page is about, normally.

Setting up alt tags differs depending on what software you are using to create your website. Normally, upon inserting an image, you will be asked what alt tag you would like to put on the image. If you are not asked to insert an alt tag, try right clicking on the image with your mouse. As with other tags, make sure you are using important keywords and keyword phrases in these tags.

Here is how to format an image with the alt tag in place:

<img src="images/keyword.jpg" width="257" height="329" alt="keywords go here.">

Header Tags:

Header tags make your words stand out in the eyes of the search engines. They also make the words large. Your header tags should be formatted like this: <h1>header<h1>. You can use numbers from 1 through 6, with 1 being the largest font possible and 6 being the smallest. Some software page editors, like Dreamweaver, let you choose the size of the font inside a header tag. Make sure you use at least one header tag inside of every page with your main keywords inside of it. You should try to use 2 header tags inside your home page and have them be of different sizes.

Strong Tag:

The "strong tag" makes words stand out to the search engine spiders. This gives you some say over regular font that you want the spiders to see as important without changing its appearance. You can also use bold, italics, and underline to accentuate words on your pages, but the strong tag is the best to use. This tag is formatted like: strong.

You should utilize these other tags throughout your content as well: <b>, <i> <u>. Those tags are for bold, italics, and underline. Use these sparingly to highlight important words throughout the content of your page.

You can't even tell by looking at them, but trust me the search engines will notice them!

Add a robots.txt file:

Open any text editor you use and insert the following:

User-agent: *

Disallow:

You can add any pages that you do not want search engines indexing after the "disallow:" command in the form of http://www.yoursite.com. Save this file into your website files and upload it to your website. Search engines look for this file. Even if you don't have to use it at this point, you should put the file in and you can add to it later.

Do not add anything you don't want any human being to find. Specifically private download addresses!

If you have a page that you don't want indexed, insert a "no index" meta tag into the page:

<meta name="robots" content="noindex">

CHAPTER 4: AN OVERVIEW

CONTENT IS KING!

Whether you are new to the Internet and SEO or someone who understands a bit about how the Internet works, the content you put onto your website is extremely important. This content consists of words necessary to convey important messages to your site visitors. By creating quality content pages, you will be naturally using your keywords and showing the search engines how important your site is.

You are an expert in your field. You know how to get the most out of your products. Why don't you explain that information to your customers? Telling your customers how to choose the right size, or pick the right color is something you should have no trouble doing.

The content of your site is extremely important to your search engine rankings. You will find that it is extremely easy to use your main keywords in content you write for your website. It is also very convenient that you are writing this content, because I will show you how to make it into links pointing to your website, which is important when attempting to get traffic.

The key to having the best content lies in your competitor's websites! Put in your main keywords in Google and take a close look at the top 10 websites. In this case (content generation) take a look at the text they have chosen to include in their web pages.

Now take a step back and think about how you can write something better for your site. Take the content you have found and put it into your own words (NOTE: copyright infringement and plagiarism will put you in the perfect position for being sued). While writing this content, improve upon everything your competitors stated. This will give you the type of content that search engines and customers are looking for.

If you end up being stuck and having difficulty finding ideas for content, search article databases and take the opportunity to read information from other experts in your field. I guarantee you will find many ideas and different articles that you didn't even think of. The main article site is Ezinearticles.com©. This is the best part about business on the Internet, there is always someone thinking of something that you haven't thought of yet!

CONTENT & INTERIOR LINKING STRUCTURE

The way that your website links to itself is important. Search engines look at the text used to link to pages and uses that information to help rank that page. Your navigation system in your website MUST consist of text links. If you use flashy navigation that spiders cannot easily read, then you should include simple text links at the bottom of your site. This ensures that the engines can find the information and pages you want them to find.

Make sure, at all costs, that your website is linked to itself using anchor text links.

The trick beyond this is to use text to link to pages in your site within the content you put together.

Adding this link with your important keywords in it, search engines will better understand how important, those words are in describing your site.

Make sure, at all costs, that your website is linked to itself using text links.

Make sure you add at least one link inside the content of each page. It will catch the eye of your customer and it will help the search engines figure out what words are important to your website and will help them rank you where you belong.

Using text links properly with the correct keywords will raise your rankings in the search engines.

It's amazing how simple this is, but it is one of the most important aspects of on-page optimization for the search engines.

There are numerous ways to implement these links into your website.

One way is to include what I call a "mini sitemap" at the bottom of each page of your website.

Another is to include links to other pages inside content you post. Either way, make sure you link to pages inside of your website when you can.

SIMPLE SITE DESIGN

The design of your site makes a major impact on two specific areas. The first is that it has to be easy to figure out for your customers. If they cannot figure it out, you will never get a sale. The second is that it has to be easy for search engine spiders to read as well. By creating a simple, easy to follow design, you will make it easier for search engines and customers to see how much of a professional you are and they will thank you for it, with sales and traffic.

Do not think of your website in SEO terms.

Think of your website as a customer would.

This is the first step in creating a profitable website. A customer must be able to easily navigate your website, to find the products and services they are looking for. The words that are found on the pages of your website greatly increase the possibility of you actually ranking for those words and phrases, so make sure you include as many words as you can on every page.

SITEMAPS

Sitemaps are your way of ensuring that search engines and customers find everything that they are looking and more importantly buying.

By adding a simple sitemap for your customers, they will have a map of your website at their fingertips.

A sitemap will make it easier for them to find what they are searching for and the search engines will pick up the links.

You must ensure that you have a regular page that is a sitemap and an xml sitemap.

Note: Use both a visual sitemap for your human customers and an XML for the search engine spiders.

XML is a language that is different from the one that we use to display a webpage and it is strictly for the search engines.

The big three search engines have all agreed to use the standard sitemap to help them index all of the pages of your website.

That means you only need one sitemap to cover them all.

Don't worry about submitting your sitemaps to search engines, simply post a link to your sitemap on your index page and they will find it.

Here is a decent sitemap builder:

http://www.xml-sitemaps.com/

For Wordpress©, use the Google Sitemaps plug-in:

http://wordpress.org/extend/plugins/google-sitemap-generator/

For more information head to:

http://www.sitemaps.org.

UNDERSTANDING WHAT WORKS AND WHAT DOES NOT:

Before you start, you must understand what is already working. If your site is active and you are making money, you need to find out how that money is coming to you. Every website host gives you tracking information, but normally it is not enough and can be very tough to decipher into something useful.

I have chosen Google Analytics$^{©}$ as my favorite statistics, tracking software, plus it is <u>free</u>.

Not only does Analytics tell you where each of your customers comes from, but lets you know what page they came from, and what keywords they used if they found you through a search engine, along with the position you held for that term.

> *Imagine how much more money you will make when your traffic triples for a keyword phrase that is already doing well for you!*

It also gives you the exact time that the customer went to your website.

This is helpful for figuring out the exact term that brought you a sale.

This information is the key to understanding where you are in the search engines and where you need to be.

If a certain keyword is bringing you in business, then you should optimize your pages for that term, especially if you are not on the first page.

If you are making money from a term on the third or fourth page of the results, then you will be able to focus your efforts and move up in ranking for those words.

Imagine how much more money you will make when your traffic triples for a keyword phrase that is already doing well for you!

LINK BUILDING THE EASY WAY!

Off page factors of search engine optimization effect ranking in the major search engines more than what your website consists of.

Here is an example of how this works

Search engines look at links to your website as votes from the site that links to yours. You could easily purchase links from websites, because there are many companies that offer this service. The problem is that most purchased links are worthless, or will negatively affect page ranking.

Here is how a link must be formatted for the best results:

<a href="http://www.ross-goldberg.com">Ross Goldberg's Immortal Marketing Blog</a>

Here is what it looks like: Ross Goldberg's Immortal Marketing Blog

The first part is the actual URL you send someone to and the second parts is the "anchor text" or words you use to link to your site. When obtaining links, you must use as many of your keywords as possible to show the search engines that these words are important to your site.

 If you put the term "click here" into Google, the Adobe® website comes up as the first result. The reason behind this is that thousands of links pointing to Adobe's website state "click here to download acrobat reader". The text on adobe.com does not have "click here" in it at all, yet they rank #1 for that term only from links pointing to their website. Now you understand how powerful the anchor text used in a link is for your website.

The links that you obtain must be from relevant sources, whenever possible. Since the beginning of the Internet, reciprocal links or link exchanges were used to add to a search engine's opinion of your website.

The search engines figured out that websites were using this method to artificially raise their search engine rankings. They have since discounted the value of an exchanged link to nearly nothing. The only time you should exchange links with a website is when it will be of value to your customers. Otherwise, don't waste time and web space for link exchanges.

A one way, inbound link offers a much higher value to your website. Websites of different sorts will provide you with very high quality inbound links and there are different types of directories that you have to utilize properly to gain inbound links for the benefit of SEO.

Here is how to use each type of site to affect your site's popularity best.

Getting .edu and .gov links: Search engines instill a huge amount of trust in these sites. Go to Google and click on "advanced search". Use your main keywords and make sure you look for sites with .edu and .gov extensions in the "Domain" area. Harvard has a list of blogs that cover nearly any subject you can imagine. Most of those blogs have something to do with law, so make your posts relevant.

Website Directories: Website directories contain links pointing to websites in many categories. When submitting to directories you have to vary your information. Your title, description, and keywords should change with every two or three directories.

Niche Website Directories: Most directories are very general, although there are some in every field of business that cater to a "type" of website. Categories include shopping, web hosting, SEO, business directories and much more. You should find some niche directories that cater to your type of business.

To find these types of directories, do a search on Google with some of your keywords and the word "directory". You get extra credit for a directory link that focuses on your field, in the eyes of a search engine.

Paid Website Directory Submissions: Paid directory submissions are the only paid for links that are not considered wrong by the search engines. As stated before, you can absolutely purchase text links from relevant sources.

These directories are extremely important when it comes to ranking well. There is a thought in the SEO Community that Dmoz[©], Yahoo, and Business.com[©] give extra benefit in the eyes of the major search engines and are absolutely must have links (Dmoz is free; the others have an annual fee).

Article Directories: This is one of the oldest link building methods on the Internet. You write an article and submit it to directories. Content publishers take your article and post it on their website. The benefit lies in the "resource box".

A resource box is the area you post the link to your website and a reason for someone to visit it. *Learn more about article marketing on page 93.*

Press Release Directories: Press Releases are an important aspect of online business. Every time you have an event, product release, redesign of your website, sale, or anything else you can think of that would be of interest to the media, you should distribute a press release. If done properly, a press release will generate a large amount of traffic and the "offline" media, which will generate even more traffic to your website, may even cover you. Every press release you put together must give a person and media personnel a reason to look further. Organize your press release like an introduction to your product, have your final product on your web page. *Learn more about press release on page 166.*

Blogging and Directories: A blog or weblog is where you can post any information about your business. Think about how many changes you have in any given week to your website. Every time you have a new sale, product, article, service, or any other reason for customers to come see your site again, you should post it to your blog. Note: an invitation into a blog directory means you must have a blog! The best blogging software option is Wordpress™. I recommend hosting a Wordpress blog on your domain. This gives you the ultimate control over your posts and can't ever be deleted. By offering good information on your blog, you will direct customers to your website. Note: Wordpress offers a hosted wordpress.com blog that is not what I am referring.

RSS Directories: Every Blog platform offers an RSS feed. You must submit your Blog's feed to RSS directories. RSS or Really Simple Syndication is another great way for you to advertise changes of your blog and website. When changes to your site occur, anyone that subscribes to it can see that there is new information and will have a reason to visit your website.

You MUST submit your RSS feed to directories. This will let search engines find you easier.

Affiliate Programs: It is simply impossible for you to find and sell to every one of your potential customers on your own. Hence, with affiliate programs, you pay advertisers to put your name out there and earn you more money in the process.

Let your affiliates do the work for you! The best part of this is the free advertising you will receive. Affiliates have to advertise your products if they want to refer new potential customers to your website and be paid for it.

Social Bookmarking Websites: The Internet is changing and web users want to voice their opinions. The idea behind social bookmarking is that you should want to share amazing websites that you use or find online. If you like it, odds are that others will like it, too.

For every site of your own that, you submit to a social bookmarking website, you must submit a valuable website you use. This puts you in the position of adding something of value for every self-serving website you add.

The key to proper Social Bookmarking is tags: Tags are words that you use to tell others about the site you submit. The best aspect of tags is that they each have their own page in a social bookmarking website. Use your best keywords as tags and your website will be listed on that tag's page. This means that you get a link to your website for every tag you choose!

Format Tags like this:

- Keyword keyword keyword

- Keywordkeyword

- Keyword-keyword

- Keyword+keyword

Forums: to use a forum properly for SEO, you must first give value to the community. The first thing you should do is try to help members of the forum, which you are involved. In a week or two, you add what is called a "signature" to your forum posts.

This signature will include a link to your website or sites. The key is to make yourself a valuable member of the community before advertising your website on a forum.

If you do not follow these simple instructions you will probably be removed from the forum permanently and lose any chance of generating links from it.

Search Engines love how forums are updated very frequently with new content.

Social Networking Websites: *My favorite networking sites are Facebook® and LinkedIn®.*

Inside a networking website, you find like-minded members that will teach you, learn from you, and even do business with you.

In each networking site, you join groups that are based on ideas you use in your business and personal life.

The level of involvement in a networking site is completely up to you.

In a nutshell:

- LinkedIn is mostly business groups.
- Facebook is all about friends.

I have dozens of people that I hadn't talked to in years find me on Facebook. By offering help to people in the groups you join, people will grow to trust you. People will then purchase from you because they trust you as an expert in your field.

Podcasts: It is important with search engine marketing and Internet business that you stay on top of current technologies.

Podcasts are basically a recording of you talking to your customers about whatever you want. I cannot even tell you how many IPods™ I see on any given day. You should make sure your podcast is visible and located in as many directories as possible.

Every single one of these options and many others are discussed in detail, later in this book.

COMPETITIVE SURVEILLANCE

When it comes to the Internet, it's highly doubtful that you'll ever be the first to do something. Nearly anything you can come up with in regards to a website has been done before.

The beauty of business on the Internet is the instant ability to test whether something will work or not.

Thousands of smart people are doing business on the web right now and the really smart ones have already tested all of your crazy ideas.

Instead of starting from scratch and having to test your own ideas, it would be very smart of you to take a very close look at your competition to see what they're doing and what they've done before.

I'm not suggesting you check your top competitor and do exactly as they've done. I'm suggesting that you look at as many of your competitors as you can and compare and contrast between what you find for each one.

This is a concept called "swiping". Taking what is already working for your competition and turning it into your own success.

You can swipe anything from the way a website is designed to the ways they are building links to their websites.

When viewing one of their websites, take a good look at the navigation of the site, the links that lead to the other pages and web properties that they own.

- How are the pages laid out?
- Are they capturing information from visitors?
- How are they doing it?
- What colors do they use?
- What product lines do they carry?
- How are they describing those products?
- What SUCKS about their sites?

If you can find something that sucks, they have left room for you to enter the marketplace and improve on their faults.

Link building surveillance tip: Here is a very simple strategy you can use to see exactly how they are getting links to point to their sites.

Go to Yahoo and search for this exact phrase: site:http://competitor.com

Also search for site: http://www.competitor.com

This will take you to Yahoo's site explorer and expose where all of the links pointing to where their websites are located.

Take a good look at how many links they have pointing to their site.

This gives you a very clear look at your competition and what you have to conquer to outrank them.

This doesn't mean that if they have 218 links and you get 219, you automatically will outrank them. The quality of every link varies and you won't be able to get the same exact links as them.

What it does give you is insight into how they're building links to their site.

Visit some of the pages that Yahoo lists as linking to your competitors.

- Where is their link located?
- Is it inside of content?
- Is it an ad?
- Is it a text link hidden on the page?

Write down the ways they are using to build links. This tells you exactly what you have to do to get similar results.

If you'd like to knock them right out of the way fast, use other methods that they haven't figured out to use!

Use instant "social" intelligence: The Internet went social over the last few years.

While there were always, different ways to communicate with others online, social networks have literally changed the way that all of us interact with each other online.

It's also changed how businesses market their products.

We're not going to go over social media marketing until later, what I want you to think about is the power of being able to watch your competitors market their businesses via sites like Twitter, Facebook, and LinkedIn.

Honestly, it is pretty simple. Figure out who the "face" of the company is. When you find who they are, become their friend on Facebook, sign up for their fan page, follow them on Twitter™, and pay attention for a few days.

What you are going to see is exactly how they are engaging their audience. You will find the exact messages they are using to market their products.

Pay attention to how they communicate. Especially note the the words they use.

Note: Remember, they were there first and what they are doing <u>is</u> working for them.

What they do might work for you, too but improving on what they are doing should be easy from an outsider's perspective (yours).

CHAPTER 5: THE ONE QUESTION

Imagine being able to see directly into the minds of your prospects. Imagine that you can see exactly what is holding them back from giving you their credit card. Imagine you know the questions in their minds and are able to answer them with ease.

You are about to figure out how to do just that!

With the social nature of today's Internet, it's easy for all of us to find people with questions about our products.

The easiest place to do this is Yahoo Answers™. (http://answers.yahoo.com)

Go to the answers site and type in your most basic keyword terms and then look through the questions.

What you are going to see is one key question being asked over and over and over again.

That is what I call "The One Question".

It's the key issue holding people back from buying what you sell. If you answer this question, it makes them feel all warm and fuzzy. Once they trust you, it's a lot easier to get them to buy from you.

Once you find the one question, answer it through the content you create and put out on the Internet to gain their attention.

Tip: Here's a very cool process you can setup that will notify you every time Google finds the mention of your "One Question".

Google has a service called Google Alerts that will send you an email every time it finds the terms you want to be notified about.

Go to http://www.google.com/alerts

Now, take a piece of your question that will give you the best results in your alerts without being too limiting.

For example, if the question is, "How do I get free traffic to my website?"

I'm going to take this piece "How do I get free traffic" and have that be my alert.

I'm also going to wrap it in quotes to be sure that I don't get a bunch of results that I can't use. By putting quotes around the term, it tells Google that I only want the results with those exact words in the exact order I specify.

Every day, I'll get a notification of new places I can go to help people, get more links, and expand my hold on my market.

Many people would tell you that all you need to do is survey your customers and prospects to gain insight into what they want. The problem is that they don't give honest answers, unless you are a survey expert and ask the perfect questions in the perfect way. With a survey, the person taking it knows that you'll be reading the answers they give you and become self conscious about what they say and how you'll perceive their answers. Plus, you have to have the attention of that audience to get them to fill out the survey in the first place.

Another cool way to gain insight into what people are thinking is to find forums in your niche.

Every market has at least one.

Inside, you'll find people talking about their issues with the same exact problems your products solve.

Of course, you can go in and answer their questions and we'll be discussing how you can do that *the right way* later in the book. The goal at this point is to simply watch and learn from what your prospects are discussing amongst themselves.

What are they saying about you, your competitors, and/or the products you sell?

What are their concerns and complaints?

These are the things you can use in your marketing to help these people and gain their attention.

CHAPTER 6: KILLER CONTENT

You heard the term "Content is King". It's true, <u>but</u> the most important details are normally being left out by those that say it.

The <u>RIGHT</u> Content is King!

What you should be doing is focusing on creating the content that will suck in visitors like crazy. Certain specific tactics will pull in visitors with little or no effort from you, outside of creating the content. These tactics are exactly what you should be focusing on.

CONTROVERSY

The term "linkbait" refers to creating the RIGHT content and here is how you do it.

Your opinion will never be the same as everyone else's. This is a good thing! You should always be checking news sites, blogs, and social bookmarking sites to see what is being discussed in your industry. Find someone with a view you disagree with and take them on.

If you have a way to comment on what they've said, do so. If you have the ability to link to your response, do that too!

What you're doing is funneling traffic from the site in question.

Do a video, write a blog post, write an article, or a press release.

Format your content to disagree, but do it honorably. *Being a jerk and calling names will make you look very stupid.* Instead, address the issue and only the issue. Your problem isn't with the person, but their ideas. Attack their ideas and not the individual.

Once you distribute this content, Make sure it is as easy to find as possible by spreading it out through your social media presence, putting it on your blog, your YouTube channel and anywhere else you can.

LISTS

This is an extremely powerful method of building traffic. I know this simply because I did it!

I created a blog at http://www.imresourcelists.com and wrote one post. This post is a list of 180 social bookmarking sites arranged by page rank. I also threw in a list of the ones that do not use the "no follow" tag. This site got over 100 visitors per day and then it dropped a bit.

The next step was to add another list. I put up a list of 64 video hosting sites and a list of tools to make creating and submitting videos easier.

This blog has gotten nearly <u>100 visitors per day</u>, every day with only <u>two posts</u>.

It is "linked to" all over the web and the traffic will explode again when I add the next list.

When creating these lists, you must strive to give the most comprehensive list available online. If others have already created these lists, go and combine what the best have done and include it in yours. <u>Do not plagiarize</u>, but feel free to use their ideas as an example.

Your lists can consist of the most read blogs in your niche, the (insert number here) ways to do (insert niche keyword here), and anything else you can come up with.

Check out Listible.com to get ideas.

TOOLS

What problems are your customers facing?

If you have, the ability create a tool or have a tool created that addresses the problem that your customers face. Create something that makes the problem either disappear or makes it easier for them to deal with it. What you create could be a Firefox® or Internet Explorer® Tool bar, desktop software, or a web based application. No matter how simple, if it works, you can expect tons of highly targeted traffic.

If you plan to sell the software, create a free version to ensure that you pull in the most interested people to your list and you will be able to contact them with follow up offers later, as well.

The key is to remember that your linkbait does not only have to go in one place. Post it to places like Squidoo™, your social networking profiles and article directories to really make a difference.

Next, social bookmark it, submit RSS feeds to RSS directories, and everything else you can come up with to get it noticed.

CREATING CONTENT, STEP BY STEP

When looking to create great content, knowing your topic is important, but writer's block can hit, too.

Lay out your content bit by bit and piece by piece. Start with your main concept. What message are you putting out?

Then, create a basic blueprint of what your content will convey. Do it by figuring out the main idea of each paragraph and laying it out.

Then, simply fill in a few sentences for each paragraph and you are done.

This method of writing will make it easier for you to put your content together quickly.

Now, you have the questions and should already know the answers to them.

How do you put your content into a format that people will enjoy?

Content is more than just text. You can use video, audio, and more to really make your content pack a punch!

**Here is a very easy way to figure out
exactly how to layout your next article,
blog post, audio, or video.**

Step 1: Figure out the main idea of your
content. What problem or question are you
going to provide the answer? Example: 4
Ways To Get Free Traffic To Your Website

Step 2: Break down how you're going to
answer that question into specific steps. You
need 4 to 6 steps for every piece of content.
Examples are Intro, Articles, Blogs, Social
Networks, and Videos.

Step 3: Flesh out each step into a simple
sentence. Example:

In this brief article, you're going to discover 4
simple ways to increase the current amount of
traffic you're getting to your website.

Articles written and submitted to popular
directories will always be the easiest way for
you to reach out to your potential visitors.

Blogs are a natural extension writing articles.

Social Networks can be fun and a very effective way to steer more traffic to your site.

The evolution of the Internet has led to videos being a common piece of the web experience for all of us.

Etc…

Step 4: Now take each sentence and add 3 more on that topic. Feel free to end this paragraph with a lead into the next one and your guide to your content is complete.

Use this guide as an article, a script for your audio or video and you're ready to rock.

To record audio, get a free piece of software called Audacity® and a plug-in called Lame©. Next, you'll need a USB microphone (you can get one for under $30 at Best Buy). Then, read your audio into your shiny new microphone. If you want to kick it up a notch, get some royalty free audio and use it for an introduction to your article. Be sure to mention your website as the "sponsor" of the audio. I'll explain exactly what to do with that audio later in the book.

Get Audacity at http://audacity.sourceforge.net/

Look on the download page at http://audacity.sourceforge.net/download/wind ows for the plugins you will need.

For video, you can get a Flip Ultra HD for under $200 and the video quality is outstanding. Get a tripod at Best Buy™ (or on Ebay if you want to save a bit). Tape your article right under the video camera on the tripod. Read the article into the video.

Again, I'll show you what to do with the video later.

74

CONTENT FOR LEADS

You'll find some additions to this book from marketing experts I've become friends with over the last few years.

This first piece comes from Alan Bechtold, he has been online since before the Internet (seriously) and has some great advice on where to find content:

Never underestimate the power of content to bring you leads.

Good content -- on your Website, in your marketing emails, in your social networking activities -- builds rapport and trust like no other traditional marketing you can do...IF you do it right.

Do it this way and generating tons of useful, keyword-rich content that is sure to get you backlinks and ranking will be easy as pie.

It helps if your niche is something you already enjoy. Are you an avid kite flyer? Great! Go after other avid kite flyers! Do you relish good cigars and seek them out to enjoy? Go after other cigar aficionados!

Just do a little research to make sure there actually ARE a good number of other people who enjoy your chosen niche and who willingly and EAGERLY spend money to enjoy it, and you've just made your life a whole lot easier.

When you focus on a niche you already enjoy, you also give yourself the authority to be an authority...because you've already been doing it for a while. Others just beginning will follow your guidance as you grow and you don't have to "fake it 'till you make it" to get recognized as a trusted authority. You just have to share what YOU found that interested YOU.

Can you see how easy this is?

Finally, make certain there are already some companies selling into your chosen niche and making a profit IN SPITE OF THEMSELVES.

This is almost always the case. If there's no competition, it's most likely not a niche worth entering. If there is competition, they almost always fail to do it right. Just study what they're doing wrong and CORRECT it for YOUR customers.

Finally -- go forth and gather. Find new information that interests you and share it on your blog, in your Tweets and on your Facebook page.

Point out resources and new products you've found and share your own personal experiences. Use personal stories and conservational text to get your points across.

 Below is a great example of sales copy that reads like a personal letter just telling stories:

http://www.DAK2000.com

Drew Kaplan does nothing more than buy the products he sells, then write compelling stories about his own experiences and ideas that he got for uses of the product while he used it himself.

Now -- go to the press release sites and search on your niche or with keywords related to your niche. Press releases are free to use and, unbelievably, there are actually still thousands of press releases still being issued for more than just the backlinks you get when they hit the distribution sites.

You can find PR distribution sites by the dozens by simply searching Google for "Press Release Distribution".

My two favorite press release distribution sites are:

http://www.PRWeb.com

http://www.PRNewswire.com

You can also find press releases on web sites that are of interest to your niche -- even direct competitors! Just look for a "PRESS" or "MEDIA" link and check it out. Usually, you can find every release the company has ever issued there, providing you with a complete history of the company and its products and the players behind them.

Grab releases about news in your niche that interest you and share what you found.

You can share the releases word-for-word, or edit them up any way you wish. Or just point to them.

Either way, you're proving your authority every time you find something new and interesting that your followers didn't find on their own.

Finally -- look at the contact information in each press release that interests you. Think about contacting that person and asking them to line up an interview with a company player.

Record the interview (stick with FIVE burning questions and it will be short, sweet and to the point), and either transcribe it or have someone transcribe it for you.

To find transcriptionists who won't destroy your budget, check out:

http://www.Elance.com

Keep Gathering all the info you can. Contact each press release issuer that you utilize and like and ask them to send you future releases directly. Then you don't have to track them down again -- they'll keep YOU informed!

The idea is to gather all you can, to find out what's happening before other people in your niche know -- and tell them.

Pretty simple -- and FUN, if you're also interested in the niche you're selling into.

This will provide you with all the keyword-rich content you could ever need to fill out your blogs, newsletters, info-products, email series and more ... without writing a word yourself, unless you want to.

You can always go through each piece you put together and (CAREFULLY) add keywords you feel would help. But I've found that truly targeted, useful information has keywords that are real to your niche and useful in building traffic for you already incorporated into them in a natural way that humans enjoy reading and the search 'bots will love as well.

--- Alan R. Bechtold

http://www.InformationPublishingPortal.com

CHAPTER 7: YOUR INDIVIDUAL STRATEGY

The final piece of preparation is to figure out what kind of time you are going to invest in your traffic strategy.

How many hours per day are you going to spend? How many days per week?

Dedicate the majority of your time to creating content and putting it out. Paying for traffic can be great and the visitors are nearly instantly coming to your website. Remember that paid traffic stops the moment you stop paying for it.

Content-based marketing will last forever.

Note: If you took 6 days per week and created 2 pieces of content per day, you'd provide over 600 new opportunities for people to find your site and buy what you sell.

A simple fact that being perceived, as "The Expert" is integral to your success in traffic generation.

Understand this first: You can become an expert in any subject, even if you currently know nothing about it. You can do this by finding information online and teaching it to yourself. This may sound difficult, but so far, I've taught myself web design, html coding, search engine optimization, traffic generation, social media marketing, copywriting, and writing as an author. If I can do all of those things, you can surely become an expert in any subject you choose!

By applying the tactics explained in this book properly, people will begin to search for you.

Every single day, I gain new customers, members of my newsletter, viewers of my YouTube® videos, and most importantly – respect from the people that learn from the information I provide. This sets me apart from my competition. I am generally respected as an honest person, someone that does their best to truly help people and provide products with the most value possible.

Never fear an informed consumer! Give the information others are afraid to share. Find the questions that your customers are asking each other about products like yours and create content that answers those questions; you will instantly become their "go to" person in your market.

You become the perceived expert by providing information most would be scared to share. Every product that anyone could sell comes with obvious objections in the eyes of any consumer. By seeing those in advance, you will be able to separate yourself from your competitors. Instead of avoiding objections, provide clarity that shows your potential customers that their objections don't apply to you.

Becoming a renowned expert in your field is easier than you might suspect. Your content must speak for itself. By providing the best information online, you will become the obvious choice for your customers.

Follow the directions contained here and you'll see your visitors increase and grow a reliable, loyal following.

My simple recommendation for this is to create a website – www.yourname.com.

This will assist with your branding.

A website with a blog will help with branding yourself and gain you exposure.

The best part is that whenever you start a new project, you can let your friends and clients know by publishing it on your website.

Many people use a Wordpress blog as their main site due to its ease of use and its customize-ability. There is an amazing array of possibilities you can do with a WordPress blog, as long as it is hosted on your site. There are hundreds of plug-ins that will add functionality to your new blog.

The next step is to handle yourself like a respectable business person. Help people! This will gain you respect and admiration among your peers and those that want to become your peers. Most people you help will become your largest supporters and you never know when they may be able to return the favor to you.

"I had a person I was mentoring that caught on so quickly, he only needed me for a few days.

I didn't speak to him for a few weeks, and then all of a sudden I received a phone call from him. He had figured out a very innovative way to earn some money online. He explained his tactic to me and honestly, it's included in this book (with his permission of course)."

This is just one example of how helping people will benefit you. Think about it!

You can become not only an expert, but also "The Expert" by spreading yourself and your content all over the Internet.

Social Media Marketing has opened doors for businesses of all sizes. You can now compete with the "WallyMarts" of the world by using smart marketing tactics that they haven't even thought of using.

Use any of the dozens of free traffic generation methods revealed here and focus on improving each one over time. As the flood of visitors grows, so will your sales and your cash flow.

I'm keeping this simple here, so follow directions and your traffic will be rolling in!

CHAPTER 8: YOUR TRAFFIC FUNNELS

Earlier (pages 17 thru 19), we talked about the search process your prospects will be using.

What we're about to go into is going to give you the insight you need for all of the different traffic generation strategies you will be using in the future.

There are other processes to consider when using traffic tactics besides what we have covered in the general overview above.

Every link to your website begins a journey for someone that clicks on it. That journey could start at any link.

How many times are you going to force someone to find a link and click on it to get to your website?

A journey of a thousand clicks starts with only one.

Will your visitors stay with you through a long journey?

Depending on the process, it can actually be helpful to put people through a few hoops to reach you. It can also cause you to lose people.

86

If someone starts at an article directory, it can lead them directly to a page on your site where they can buy something, but that's not your only option.

You could also lead to a blog post where they can find more information on the same topic.

Visitors could be directed to the index of your site, but you could also lead them to an inner page of your site where they can immediately purchase a product that solves the problem addressed in the content you wrote.

Always keep in mind the amount of control you have with the content you post online.

Most sites (article directories, hosted blogs, and video sites) have specific limits they place related to how many links you can put in the content and where those links are supposed to go.

Article directories will want you to put your links inside your resource box.

Hosted blog sites give you a lot of control and let you choose how to setup your content, but Squidoo© and Hubpages© limit how many links you post.

You need to test as many different "traffic funnels" as you can by linking to different properties you own.

Try linking to a blog post with expanded ideas from article directories. Then, inside the blog post, you can setup links to places to purchase from you inside of your content, at the end of your content, and inside sidebars.

There are literally dozens of ways to lead into the sales process. See what leads to the most sales and creates the most profits for you.

CHAPTER 9: THE MOST IMPORTANT DETAIL...

Instead of a "do this" type of idea, this is more of a "never forget this" situation.

As you get more traffic, you will get more sales and make more money.

There is a specific pitfall that I watch most of my friends fall into and I want to do my best to protect you from.

Remember, every visitor to your site is a person and came for a reason.

Statistics begin to outshine the fact that you're dealing with human beings.

You'll be able to figure out exactly how much money each visitor is worth to you.

While this information is valuable and something you should definitely figure out, don't forget that every visitor to your site is a person and came for a reason.

If they leave without buying, you didn't provide the solution they needed.

If you do provide their solution and they don't purchase from you, you didn't convey that you can help them in the way that would have them buying what you sell.

Always keep your processes at the front of your mind.

Watch websites of your competitors and take notes on what you can implement to your own business to improve your sales rates and conversion for a visitor to a customer.

The next section is a checklist that will help your succeed in your action plan. Everything in the checklist has been covered in previous chapters so feel free to go back and re-read sections above to clarify your action plan.

SECTION ONE: ACTION PLAN CHECKLIST

☐ **Do your keyword research.**

Use the worksheet at thewebtrafficbook.com and choose your primary and secondary sets of keywords.

☐ **Research your competition.**

How are they marketing their businesses? What can you do better than they can?

☐ **Adjust your on page settings to boost your rankings.**

Change image names to reflect your keywords used in alt tags, use your title tag to reflect what your page is about (and use your keywords), use heading tags to emphasize important terms.

Never forget that your visitors need to be able to read and understand your pages if you want them to buy anything from you.

☐ Plan your persona.

Who are you going to be to your marketplace? What stance are you going to take on important issues?

Figure out who you are going to be to your audience by finding what they need and conveying that you are the solution to their problems.

☐ Begin creating as much content as you can.

You're going to need it.

Check back to page 75 to find Alan Bechtold suggests for CONTENT FOR LEADS

☐ Read the rest of the book.

Get started now but keep reading…

SECTION TWO: SOLID STRATEGIES

This part of the book goes over all of the tactics you should be doing to attract people to your websites more extensively then the overview earlier in Chapters 1 through 9.

Many of the strategies allow you to build links pointing to your websites. These links act as "votes" in the viewpoint of search engines, so you'll want to get as many as you can.

You've done your research, you are following the action plan checklist and should be ready to actively work to reach new people.

Always keep your keywords, in the back of your mind with any marketing you do. The more types of sites you have links from, the better.

This next section will cover topics previously mentioned more extensively and covers new material that is important to you for success so as you complete your action plan and start moving forward read on to gain real in-depth understanding of what you need.

CHAPTER 10: ARTICLE MARKETING

Writing articles and submitting them to article directories is one of the oldest ways to create quality links to your website.

The concept is simple: You write good content concerning the topics that fit your products and are allowed to include a resource box at the end with a link to your website. You submit your article to article directories and other webmasters will take that article and publish it on their website.

Article Marketing is the most effective method of advertising I use for a few specific reasons:

- It costs absolutely nothing (except your time).

- Establishes your professionalism, expertise, and knowledge in your industry.

- Some of the highest quality links you can get are from the top article directories.

Writing articles should be easy for you if you revert back to the content creation method, we outlined a few chapters back (page 70).

You know your products well enough to write about what they will do for someone.

Always focus on the benefits your products provide to their users.

Think of what the consumer needs to know about your products.

You should easily be able to come up with 10 or more ideas about articles you could write.

Here are sources for when your ideas run out:

- Forums in your niche – pay attention to the questions being asked. Odds are that others are wondering about that same question.

- There are hundreds, if not thousands of article directories online, but www.ezinearticles.com is the most well known. This is important, because you can get ideas for articles by reading ones that are already there. Don't plagiarize, but get ideas from articles that have been written.

- Your competition's websites! Check the content on your competition's site. If they have great content, recreate it **in your own words** and distribute it.

- Blogs! Use your main keywords and the term "blog" and take a look at what people are talking about in your area of expertise. Check the comments on posts and the ones with the most comments are the common questions that need to be answered.

Thinking outside of the box is what will separate you from the others competing with you.

Here are a few things I do that most of my competitors don't:

- E-zines – Look for popular e-zines and check their index page for a "submit article" link. You could have your article distributed to thousands for free. Normally they will also publish your article on their website, providing you with a link to your website.

- Forums – Most forums include an area for articles. This is another great way to get your possible customers to find your information and realize that you are a genius and they need to spend money at your website.

Distributing your articles is a necessity to gain the best exposure. My favorite four article sites are:

www.ezinearticles.com
www.goarticles.com
www.articlesbase.com
www.articledashboard.com

Your articles must be written to pull in the reader, if you want the most traffic from your efforts. One way to do this is to write a series of articles and put additional information on your blog or your website. Link to this additional content in your resource box of the article and tell the reader to "go here" to get more information. Since you control your own website, you can advertise anything you want on that page.

There are hundreds of other ways to motivate a reader to visit your site.

Be creative and you'll have more visitors.

I have a **secret recommendation** regarding these sites to truly set apart your results.

Test different resource boxes! To do this you must submit the same article to all 4 of the top sites with varied resource boxes. Track which resource box gets the most clicks. Once you have those results, use the one that gets the most clicks for a full distribution.

THE NEXT LEVEL OF ARTICLE MARKETING

Writing articles and submitting them is old school. Don't get me wrong, it still works extremely well. What can we do with an article now that couldn't be done before?

Turn your article into a video! Take your article and break it down into bullet points. You can do this by taking the most important points and making them as simple as possible. Grab some images from any stock or royalty free image service you like to use. Go into any graphics program and make all of the images the same size.

Next, type your bullet-points right on the images. Find some decent background music or use a microphone to narrate your video yourself. You now have a video article that you can distribute to all of the video services. You can to include a watermark with your website address or a call to action at the end of your video.

An article that is well written can be turned into any number of different things.

The first question to ask yourself is what you want your article to achieve for you.

- Do you want it up for some extra links for SEO purposes?

- Are you looking to get more traffic?

- Would it be OK if it went viral?

Once you figure out what you need your article to accomplish, think about what else you could do with the ideas presented in your article. Here are some options for you:

- Could you turn it into a viral style Ebook to promote your products?

- Is the content good enough to become a blog post (the answer to this should almost always be yes)?

- Would this work well as a spoken podcast?

Do you have a bunch of articles on one topic? If not, you will soon. When you do, think about what it would take for you to combine those articles and create a book.

Your book can be one that is found in bookstores or something digital. It depends on what your content says to you when you put it together. Keep an open mind and be prepared to put in a little effort. Apply your ideas and watch your content spread across the web.

CHAPTER 11: VIDEO MARKETING

VIDEO MARKETING WORKS.

With video marketing, conversion rates from prospect to sale are higher. Businesses are reaching more people on a deeper level than any simple web page or email could.

When you use video, it is engaging to the viewer.

Think back on how the Internet was a few years ago. Every web page was static. That means that it simply sat there. You could look at a page, read the contents, and move on when you were finished.

Now, the web is interactive and engaging. People are giving input all over the web on any imaginable subject through blogs, social networks, social bookmarking and of course, video.

Let's take a look at why video is so important.

Video, unlike text, allows you to actively engage your audience. The uses of video are unlimited. The only thing stopping you from coming up with the next amazing idea is your mind and ideas (and the fear of using them).

Here are some uses for video to get you thinking:

- Sales videos to improve conversion on sales pages.

- Tutorials to find new customers and improve info products.

- Branding videos to show how much of a nice person you are.

- Commercials advertising your products.

- Introducing a new product.

- Image slide shows to pull out a particular emotion.

- Powerpoint® presentations to teach.

- Family videos to show how "real" you are.

- Etc...

These are simple ideas that have been applied over and over again. Be creative and come up with something special. It will only bring more attention to you and your business.

Knowing how to make high quality videos is great, but what if your customers don't like them?

That creates a huge problem for you. Here you are, after applying a bunch of your time to create these videos for your customers, yet they don't appreciate them and also don't buy your product.

That sucks!

You need to take the proper angle when branding your company and creating content for your customers.

To get ideas, you need to either **ask your customers**, or find where your customers hang out and eavesdrop.

By allowing your customers to tell you what they want, you remove the possibility of failure with your videos.

The last thing you need or want is to spend your time for nothing.

So, listen to your customers and give them what they want.

What you need to be thinking about is very similar to how you would write copy for a sales piece.

A = Attention

I = Interest

D = Desire

A = Action

Applying copywriting rules to your writing or video creation process is as simple as keeping the needs of your prospects at the forefront of the content you use to market your business.

- How do you connect with your audience?
- What is the main piece missing from their puzzle?
- What will it take for you to show that you relate to their largest problems and frustrations?
- Most importantly – How do you show you have the solution?

Connecting with your audience is based upon them relating to you. What is your story? Have they gone through something similar? Even if they haven't been through similar things, showing that you're a human being will go far with any of your customers.

How do you find what they are missing? This was answered for you in the last video above. Find their questions and provide answers.

How can you show that you relate? Passion. Passion. Passion. If you get angry over something that frustrates your audience, run to grab your camcorder and record your thoughts. Edit the video and show it to them. You are now human in their eyes.

There are other people attempting to steal your customers out from under you right now. They are different from you and may be doing better marketing. If they steal your customer, it isn't their fault. It's yours!

Showing the solution is done by giving small pieces of the puzzle. You take a few pieces of the puzzle and give it away. When you do this, you are helping people hoping that they will see you and your solution as the one they need.

Never be afraid of revealing your secrets to your customers. There should be no secrets between you. You're just going to have them pay you for the whole picture.

The most effective method of reaching a customer is social proof.

It's one thing for you to say how amazing you are, but it's totally and completely different for someone else to say it.

Anybody can write a few paragraphs about themselves and tack on a picture of some random person with a goofy name and location.

What if you used a video testimonial?

There is no doubting that this person is real and they can convey their emotion in the words they use, their facial expressions, and the inflection of their voice.

It's simply real.

By incorporating this into a sales page or promotional video, it can make a huge difference in the amount of sales you make and people that are interested in you and your products.

What else?

Visual proof.

If you claim that something made you a large amount of money, you should show that amount in something that can be seen. Pictures can be doctored, but videos are much harder to tweak.

A video is more believable than an image, as an image is more believable than a claim in passing.

The more solid your proof, the more believable it is.

For anyone to be interested in your business and your services, you must show them why they should be interested at all. Proof (social or visual) makes it much easier to trust you.

The true power of video is to make huge impact with very little work.

My best videos have been made when I was pissed off about something and put together a video in a period of five minutes.

I spoke my mind. There were no notes, there was no sheet to read from and nobody was there making sure I said anything specific.

The more natural you appear in your videos, the better. Relax, take some deep breaths and remember that you can always delete the one you are recording and start over.

My videos that have received the most positive response (and gotten the most views on YouTube) had simple Camtasia© screen captures of my computer screen showing how to do something related to Internet marketing. I still get compliments on them every day (one has nearly 80,000 views, which is unheard of in my market).

Some had been advertising something, but most were not. They were simply there to help people and that is what they have done.

It's funny, but the videos that have made the most difference for my business have been the ones that didn't advertise anything at all.

Do you think the value of a subscriber goes up when they have to search for you to sign up for your list, instead of having a blatant ad thrown in their face? Think about it...

The secret to creating great videos is in the content.

You could create a video and upload it immediately to YouTube™.

What if you want to make it look cool?

What if you screw up while recording?

What if you want to do a screen capture of your computer?

What if you want to do some really cool stuff with video?

You would have to be able to edit the video and I'm going to show you how! I am going to answer all of the questions above.

Here is what you need to record a great video:

- An idea.

- Something to capture it.

Nice and easy, right? **Not so fast!**

Here are the methods you can use to create killer videos with ease.

- A recording of you talking/acting.

- A screen capture of what you're doing.

- An image slide show.

- A presentation.

- Totally crazy videos.

Would you believe that the image quality of your personal videos is actually unimportant?

Seriously, some of the most popular videos are of a horrible quality and they still get tons of views and a huge amount of people talking about them.

I use a simple Flip Camera to record most of my videos. Their HD Flip Ultra is right around $200. I recently purchased a Kodak Zi8 due to it having an audio input (which greatly increases audio quality through a high quality microphone).

I import the videos into Sony Vegas and edit them with ease.

The first piece of doing your live videos is proper lighting.

Your goal is to make it look natural and ensure that viewers can see all that is important.

Here is an image to help you better picture how to setup your lighting.

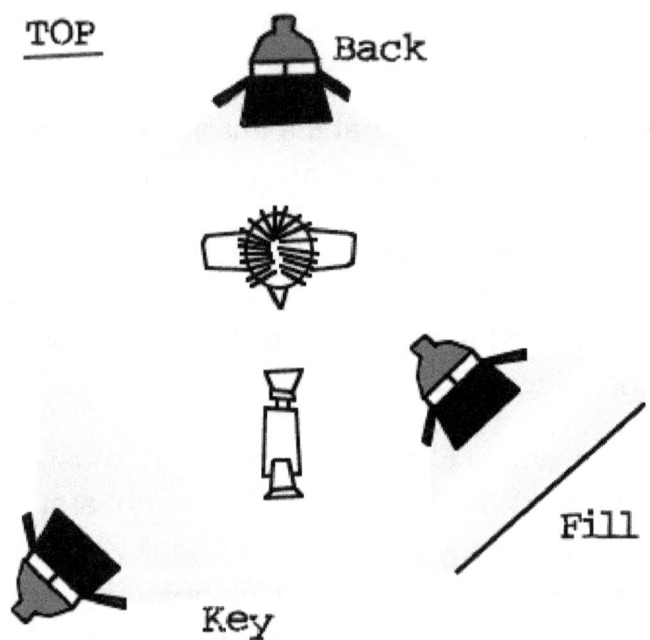

The back light should be above or below your main subject.

The key light should be above pointing down.

The fill light must shine on a reflective surface to fill the room with light. You can do this with something as simple as aluminum foil.

Check your local discount stores for fluorescent lights that you can buy for $50 or less. You want power, but you don't want to pay $2000 for the lighting for your videos.

If your lights shine too brightly, cover them with a simple white cloth to soften the light. **Warning:** Be very careful with this! Hot lights, plus flammable cloth can equal fire. Be sure that any cloth is at least a few inches from the hot light bulb.

If they are not bright enough, return them and get brighter ones!

Try not to focus your main lights directly on your subject. You should have one light on each side of it to reduce shadows.

Test your lights to ensure that you are happy with the way your subject looks.

When you first start, you will definitely not be an expert, so take your time and you will become a pro before you know it!

Here is a great example of an inexpensive lighting setup.

Notice how the lights are pointed upwards. The ceiling reflects the light downward making it well lit and it looks natural.

The white backdrop is professional and allows the focus to be the subject.

Remember that the best lighting is from the sun. It is natural, so it looks that way.

What if you switched out the white backdrop for a green screen?

Then, you could create your own professional looking green screen video.

With a green screen, you can insert any image or video behind you and create a totally new feel for your video.

People pay as much as $2000 for this simple effect (hint, hint...).

To get your backdrop, go to a simple craft store and get a large piece of green felt. The important aspect is the color, not the actual material.

A normal green screen costs as much as $200 for the simple material, so save yourself most of that by using green cloth instead.

Here are some tips to guarantee your success in creating the best video possible.

- Be sure to setup your camcorder a good distance between you and the background. You should be about 4 feet in front of the screen if possible to avoid the possibility of shadows being in your video.

- Place your lights behind your camcorder to be able to focus your lighting in the best way possible.

- Find your background before doing your video, so you understand exactly how its going to look when you're done.

- **Find free, public domain video backdrops at** Archive.org.

- You can find royalty free music by searching "royalty free music" on Google.

- When using free music or video, be sure to check your rights so you don't get into legal trouble!

- If you need a script or bullet points to keep you focused and on task during your video, get a large white piece of cardboard at your local discount store and place it directly behind your camcorder.

  This will make it look natural if you have to refer to your notes while recording.

Screen capture videos are very powerful.

You can teach anything that you can personally do on your computer to others (great for creating information based products).

To do your screen captures, I strongly recommend Camtasia. The best part about this software is that they offer a 30 day trial. This means that you can download it, use it, and make it pay for itself.

Before doing a screen capture, the best thing you can do is setup what you are going to do before recording.

Being setup properly is important. Open multiple tabs on your Internet browser and check the sites you'll be referring to before you record anything.

The best screen captures are not scripted. You must use voice inflection to show your emotion and what you are thinking. Many screen capture videos are horrible and you don't want anyone thinking that yours fall into the "horrible" category. If you need a script of some sort, write down bullet points for an outline you can follow.

Don't hesitate to show your personality in your videos. Be engaging.

You can, and should, record literally anything you can do online or on your desktop. Technically difficult or confusing tasks are especially interesting to people.

Don't forget how to find ideas and subjects for your videos. This applies here, just like everywhere else.

Image slide shows are the easiest videos to create.

They can also be the most boring.

Here is how you can make sure yours aren't putting your customers and potential customers to sleep.

The first step is to get some royalty free music. You can find it by simply searching Google.

I strongly recommend using Audacity to mix your audio. It's extremely easy to use and it's also free. You'll need the Lame plugin to export your files as MP3s.

I also recommend picking up a decent USB microphone to get the best possible audio quality. You can get them at Best Buy for under $30.

Simply import your music and let it play for the intro piece of your audio. I recommend only letting it last for 15 seconds or so. Talk over it to introduce what your video is about. Then lead the viewer through the message you want to give them and link your images to each part of the audio that applies to it.

Next, go to File and click "Export as MP3" and you have your audio finished.

Pick up images by searching for "Royalty free photos" on Google. Write over the images using any graphics software you may use. You need to engage your video viewer, so make sure you use fonts and colors that attract attention.

At the end of the video, provide your URL and you're all done.

Windows PCs have a software called Windows Movie Maker[®] that makes this process very simple. Mac[®]s have IMovie[®] and it's also very easy to use.

Creating a presentation is actually very easy.

Camtasia automatically plugs into Microsoft Powerpoint where you can record directly from that software.

If you don't use Powerpoint®, it's a touch more difficult, but it's also free.

Open Office is an office suite that is nearly as powerful as Microsoft Office® and it has its own version of Powerpoint called Impress.

With Powerpoint, simply choose a background and set up your presentation. Camtasia will automatically switch it into a slide show for you to record the presentation with ease. Set up your microphone and start recording.

With Impress®, you have to set your screen size and begin recording before starting your slide show. You will have to edit out the first few seconds before the slide show begins.

With a presentation, be careful to give yourself room to talk and add to the presentation itself. Your ideas should be free flowing, while the presentation guides you through your video and keeps you on task.

Also, avoid fancy graphical transitions. They normally look very bad and make your video look unprofessional. Leave them out and let your content and ideas make your presentation that much better.

The content of your presentation totally depends on what you are teaching. Focus on the core elements in the presentation itself to keep people paying attention and listening to what you have to say.

Avoid any sales information until you have put out enough content to keep the attention of any of your viewers. Include a simple watermark of a URL or wait until the end of the video to suggest that your viewer goes to the page you are recommending.

The best thing about video is that you can do things that nobody else has thought of in your field. Becoming a video expert isn't necessary if you have the tools at your disposal to create fun and interesting videos.

All you have to do is find the right software and you can literally create anything and make yourself look like an expert with very little effort.

My favorite software for creating special videos is Crazy Talk you can find it at http://www.youtalkcrazy.com/.

It animates still images with any voice you add to it and creates some amazing possibilities for your video marketing. All you need is a still image and a voice to create anything you can dream up.

Would you believe that any video editing trick you could need should already be available on the web or YouTube?

I've given you my tips and tricks, but every time I get stuck, I do a search on YouTube or Google to find my answers.

This book is not meant to be the end all guide to creating video and you'll find the answer to nearly any video editing question for free on YouTube when you get stuck.

It's time to turn off the TV, lock the doors, and focus on the most important piece here:

Content + Mystery + Call to Action = Profits

- Your content must answer a question related to what you are promoting.

- Mystery is a necessity for causing the

122

viewer to feel the urge to find out more about your subject.

- You must tell them specifically what you want them to do. Go to a website? Sign up for a list? Buy something? Let them know and they might just do it.

You can do this with any method of creating your videos. It doesn't matter how it was made.

What does matter is your call to action and branding.

How can you brand every video as yours with ease?

Create a watermark. To do this, go into your photo editing software and create a clear background that is the size of your video (normally 640 X 480 pixels). Now, post your logo to the lower right of the image. Make it roughly 50% transparent and you're all set.

Once you get your video done you want to get as many people to see it as possible.

YouTube is the most popular video site online. The average amount of time a user spends on YouTube is 43 minutes per day (seriously).

What if I told you that you could show up immediately after nearly any video on YouTube that you wanted? When a YouTube video ends, it shows a group of similar videos. Here is how you can make your videos show up after any other on the site.

You need to follow this formula to make it happen:

1. Use the same tags in your video in the same order as the one you want to show up after.

2. Use the same main terms in your title and descriptions.

3. Send traffic to your video.

Send your subscriber list to your video on YouTube to boost the views. Traffic is the only piece that may cause you a touch of trouble.

The more views you get, the better the odds of showing up right after your targeted video.

Viral video began out of a natural evolution of the web. With everyone interacting more, it was only natural that certain content get passed around the Internet at record speeds.

The first viral video that I personally remember was the Star Wars Kid (http://www.youtube.com/watch?v=HPPj6viIB mU). His original video was pretty stupid, but amusing. The cool part came when experienced video editors took his original video and turned it into something visually fun.

This video has over 16 million views and most of the ones that used his video have millions of views, too.

It went viral all by itself. These videos that "just happen" to go viral are great, but what if you could push a video to go viral?

You can and should.

The best method is to give something of value in exchange for having someone recommend your site to everyone else.

Motivation is key and a necessity to force a viral wave of visitors and viewers to your videos.

The next piece is to do something truly revolutionary. If you do something amazing, the viral aspect will come naturally.

Getting your videos watched on YouTube is one thing, but what about getting ranked in the search engines?

I have top ranking for 5 extremely competitive terms on Google video. Here is how I did it:

Getting viewers to your video is actually very simple. Use the keyword terms you are targeting on YouTube to find other videos on the same subject.

Leave comments that are relevant and not "spammy".

Make friends and join groups to find more like-minded people.

Create video responses to the videos that are similar to yours.

YouTube is a video-based social networking site, so socially network on YouTube!

Now, simply try to reach more people and your videos will get more views and you will have more fans.

Video SEO Secret: As discussed earlier, links are the main thing to concern yourself with when it comes to search engine optimization. Once my video is done, I embed it into one or more of my blogs. Directly below my video, I place an anchor text link back to the video on YouTube using the keywords I targeted inside the title, description, and tags I used when I originally posted the video.

Video Editing Secret: When you get stuck while editing your videos, go to YouTube and type in what you're trying to do and the software you're trying to do it with: Example - "Sony Vegas green screen". When it comes to simple technical issues, you can almost always find the solution or a shortcut on YouTube. The site is perfect for things like this, just don't go there looking for strategy advice!

CHAPTER 12: BLOGGING

Having your own blog is an absolute necessity. A blog or weblog is a website you can easily update and post to on a daily basis to keep your customers and potential customers know what is going on in your business, industry, and even you personally. Blogging is a simple art that must be mastered to keep your customers informed and generate more traffic and income for your company.

You can set up your blog with a blogging service like Blogger.com or you can set it up on your own hosting plan. The best choice for blogs on your website is Wordpress. The reason I recommend Wordpress is that it is easily customizable. You can install plug-ins to make your blog original and the experience more enjoyable.

Start off with providing articles you have written about your niche. Post an article every day for your first week online. After this you can pepper in promotional posts between articles. The articles are a way to drive visitors and once you get them there, you can do some minor promotion. This is not a way of direct advertising. Keep your blog posts as informational as you can. Subtlety will get you everywhere with a blog. If someone senses advertising, they will click away before you get a chance to sell them on your products.

The content you provide will dictate how many readers you get.

Typical things they love are top lists (7 ways to make more money in less time), controversy, gossip, anything funny, and other topics that will pull out their emotions.

Once you build a following, be sure to make it easy for your visitor to access your products and services. You can post them to their own page, but also include links to them in your sidebar. That way they are available on every single page of your blog.

If you don't have a lot of them, use some affiliate programs. You can also find advertisers and allow them to post an image or text link on your blog.

To find out what to charge, check other blogs and see what they charge for ads.

You want to find blogs with similar traffic to yours and once you find them, request an advertising quote. Be sure to request more than one blog and compare the rates of as many as you can find.

Charge your rates based upon the average price that your competition has setup.

There are numerous widgets you can use on your blogs sidebar.

Widgets like Twitter, MyBlogLog, Facebook and tons of others.

There are thousands of plugins and widgets you can use on your blog.

Be sure to focus on your social presence and the ability for readers to spread around your ideas. **Avoid things like games on a business style blog.**

To really get ridiculous results, you should not only start one blog, but come up with a few sub-blogs you can set up.

Your main blog should be a Wordpress blog hosted on your own hosting plan (installation instructions are above).

Your other blogs should be hosted by different sites (blogger, MySpace, typepad, Xanga, etc...). This allows you to create an inner linking structure and pass visitors back and forth between your own blogs.

Do <u>very</u> focused topics for sub-blogs and a wider topic for your main one.

Secret Tip: What do you think it would do if you posted on the best blog in your niche?

I'm not talking about a comment, but a guest post as a writer.

Create something unique that would appeal to the audience of any of the top blogs in your market and send it to the owner of the blog. If you can guest post on their blog, it will build your reputation and get you tons of targeted traffic.

WHAT IS RSS?

RSS stands for "Really Simple Syndication". Every blogging software comes with an RSS feed. This RSS feed allows people that like your blog to be automatically updated every time you post to your blog. It's totally and completely automatic.

The most important benefit of having RSS feeds is that every time you make a new post to your blog, you'll automatically get new links from any site that has your feed listed. Adding your RSS feed to RSS directories is a necessity for any feed you own.

You can create an RSS feed for any of your main websites. Syndicate your articles for your customers and host it on your website. Create a feed for new products. You can literally put anything in a feed that you update often.

Get an RSS feed creator for free at http://sourceforge.net/projects/rssfeedcreator

Your RSS feed includes a title, description, and link for every item. Be sure to use attention getting titles to generate actual traffic from your RSS feed. Use important keywords in titles for SEO purposes.

Secret Tip: RSS feeds come with all types of blogs and websites you'll be using to generate traffic. Here are sites that give you RSS feeds you can submit to get more links:

- Every Social Bookmarking Service

- Myspace

- Twitter

- Squidoo

TWITTER

The first thing you should do as a new twitter user is to set up your profile, so that those visiting your page see that you are active within the community and are far more likely to follow you.

One of the biggest mistakes that new twitter marketers make is in immediately adding contacts to their following list, without having issued out tweets, updated their profile or uploaded a photo of themselves.

This makes sense if you already have an online presence and are simply incorporating your current contacts from your address book or mailing list, but if you are currently working to establish your brand or grow your business, it's critical that you develop your twitter presence first, and then add or invite new followers.

This begins with your profile page, the entry point that every potential follower visits prior to adding you as a contact.

You need to make sure that you complete your profile and that you provide useful information about yourself so that people can either identify you, or at the very least, know what you are offering, are involved in or are interested in.

There are a few different fields relating to your profile that should never be left out, including your full name and your website URL.

Since your username becomes part of your twitter profile's URL, you should also make sure that you use a username that is relevant to your market, niche or represents your business.

You can choose to use your name, if it's available for registration, your website URL, business name or simply keywords representing the market you are involved in.

Personally, I recommend that if at all possible, use your full name as your twitter username, so that your profile URL is structured like this:

http://twitter.com/Jane-Doe

or

http://twitter.com/JaneDoe

One thing that a lot of people don't know is that the keywords featured within your actual twitter profile URL tie directly in with twitters built in search utility, meaning that whenever someone searches for information using specific keywords, twitter searches through profiles and usernames to pull relevant search results.

This means that you should always include your primary keywords within your profile fields, including your bio area, so that you are far more likely to be included in search results each time someone enters in a relevant keyword associated with your market.

It's important to determine what brand you are creating on twitter. If you run multiple websites or businesses, use different names (pen names) or business names, you will need to consider the best approach to take.

Do you want to create a single twitter account that serves as an all-in-one contact center for your different markets, or is it better to create multiple twitter accounts, each one focusing on your different businesses and markets?

Even with twitter's simplistic structure, and the vast amount of tools that are available to help automate your activity and in building a following, you'll still need to spend time actively participating within the twitter community, if you want to further your business and maximize your exposure.

This can be exceptionally difficult to do if you are running and managing multiple twitter accounts, so take that into consideration when you are developing your twitter account and choosing your main focus.

From personal experience, I find that by separating my tweets and activity for each of my main markets helps keep things organized and on track.

I manage four different twitter accounts, each serving a different community base, covering mainstream Internet marketing to micro niche subjects.

Since the topics I cover are so different, the only way to successfully market my services via twitter, was to create multiple accounts that run independently from each other.
This also allows me to send out multiple tweets (messages) for each of my markets, rather than confusing potential buyers by using one account that randomly broadcasts messages covering multiple niches.

Twitter has absolutely no problem with people opening up multiple accounts, however you must actively use these accounts in order to keep them.

If you allow an account to go dormant and un-used for a period of time, twitter reserves the right to terminate the account and open up the possibility of someone else registering that username, so if you do intend on creating multiple twitter accounts, make sure that you log in regularly to keep them active.

From within your twitter account, you will be able to add in a short bio. This field is exceptionally important! Once again, with twitters search function, it pulls information from users' bios to match them up with keywords entered into the search engine.

This means that you should include keywords that are relevant to your niche market, so that you are able to maximize exposure by being included in search results whenever another twitter user enters in those keywords.

Your bio shouldn't showcase just keywords, however. You also want to ensure that you provide a bit of information about yourself, so that people who aren't familiar with you can get to know who you are, and consider following you.

Your bio field, just like any twitter broadcast you send out, is also limited to only 140 characters, so you'll need to take some time to determine the best terms to describe yourself and your business.

Separate keywords with comma's so that each keyword is individually placed:
Example: Social marketer, writer, online business, speaker

There are other settings that you can configure to suit your preferences, and to help you with the twitter commands and other customization options, I've included a 'Twitter Handbook" in the zip file from this package, so be sure to go through it and make sure that your twitter account is set up and tweaked before going any further.

When you are satisfied with your account, it's time to write your first tweet! This can make people a little anxious, especially since once you post a tweet, everyone who visits your profile or chooses to follow you will be able to see it.

With twitter, if you ever want to delete a message that you previously sent out, all you have to do is click on the tweet, look for the trash can icon and click it, to delete your message from the time line.

There is also the option to mark specific tweets as favorites, which will make it easy for you to locate that tweet later on, once you have multiple messages in the time line.

When it comes to writing tweets, don't spend a lot of time worrying about whether it's creative enough, witty enough, or interesting enough.

Once you have become an active member of the twitter community, you'll find it easier to think of entertaining and useful tweets, and will also be able to respond to ongoing discussions from those you follow and who follow you.

For now, post whatever's on your mind. Working on a website? Post about it. Perhaps you've found an interesting website or news story, post about it.

The idea is to simply post enough so that you become comfortable with the twitter system, and more importantly, so that your profile page shows activity before you start inviting people to follow you.

Once you've posted your first tweet, it's time to start following people on twitter, so that you can build up your twitter presence, and encourage people to follow you in return.

Don't just sign up and blast out ads every few minutes expecting to achieve anything but annoying those on your list.

Take the time to talk to people individually by directing messages to specific people, post useful information or links to free products and resources that people in your various niche markets would appreciate.

Just like anything else you need to develop a reputation on Twitter as being someone who is interested in helping others, while developing your own Twitter presence.

A great thing about Twitter is the ability to quickly locate other people who are involved in your target market, or industry.

For example, if you are looking to find people to interview who may be experienced in specific things, you can find many people who are involved in nearly every topic and subject online.

It's like a rolodex of the entire online business industry, and as Twitter continues to grow, more and more people are jumping on board, so expect to see Twitter evolve and change to improve their system and add more interactive, productive features that will make it even easier for use to reach out to other users.

Posting subtle little updates about your current projects, websites, blogs and products is an easy way to keep people up to date on what you are doing, even people who otherwise might not know who you are, or what you do.

The way you present your updates, and the frequency in which you do it, (avoiding Twitter spamming) is critical in staying current and helping your brand become memorable, and noticed by the community.

Growing your following on Twitter is a simple process. Now that you know the basics, all you have to do is hang out and talk to others in your market. They're already on Twitter, so send them a message by including their username with the "@" sign before it, like this: "@rossgoldberg I am in the middle of reading your book and I love it, thanks for putting together such a great resource!" As you have your conversations with these people, people that follow them will begin to follow you. This strategy takes time, but it works. Use it!

Remember our "linkbait" piece from earlier in the book? Rather than posting a link to a direct news story, post a summary of it on your blog and direct people to your page in order to read the message you are broadcasting.

This is a passive aggressive marketing tactic that works very well within twitter, because rather than directly trying to sell to your following base, you are simply posting about something you found interesting, useful or entertaining.

Once you have them on your blog, they'll likely explore your website and if you've done your job of developing relationships with your following base and staying active within the twitter community, it will be a lot easier to convince them to subscribe to your newsletter or purchase your products.

Connecting with your followers is one of the most important aspects of a successful twitter marketing campaign, and the more you do it, the easier it is to direct people to your website each time you post a new message, launch a new product or are simply looking for feedback on a potential project.

I've seen marketers directly asking their following base to critique their website, complete a survey or poll in order to generate feedback, to test drive a new script they developed or beta test their software.

Because they have worked to develop relationships with their followers by staying active within the twitter community, offering helpful advice or information, the response they receive whenever they directly ask their following base to visit their website, is phenomenal.

People pay attention to their broadcasts, they visit their websites regularly, and they click on every link sent out within their tweets simply because they spent the time developing an active twitter presence and more importantly, gave back to the community first.

When it comes to generating traffic from twitter, you need to be willing to put in the work of first developing a history on the network itself.

This means that rather than instantly start posting tweets directing potential followers to your website, you want to fill up your time line with personal tweets, that are not focused on selling, but instead, focused on letting people learn more about you.

Once you've done that, those visiting your profile page will see your recent activity and that you have been consistently active over time, and are focusing on being part of the community, rather than just promoting your own business.

If you do that, you will be able to grow an active following base who will pay attention to your tweets and subsequently, respond to your messages and click on the links that direct them to your website.

It's as simple as that. People try to over complicate the entire process of marketing on twitter, but what it all comes down to is developing relationships first, a business second.

You want your twitter account to represent you, who you are, where you're from, what you are interested in so that you are able to successfully connect with potential buyers on a more personal level than with direct marketing.

Once you have a presence on twitter and are interested in directing people to your website, you should use twitter's current discussions as potential topics for your blog posts. What better way to create curiosity, or address your following base directly than by writing about what they are currently interested in?

By browsing through the time line of your entire following base, you will be able to instantly come up with a lot of fresh, new ideas on what to blog about.

Furthermore, it's a lot easier to generate traffic to your website when you are able to post a link to a message that addresses a current discussion.

After all, that shows you are paying attention to discussions, are interested in the same topics, and are willing to participate in the community.

If you are interested in developing a presence as an expert or authority in your niche, creating blog posts that address questions or discussions currently taking place within your following base is an exceptionally easy way to help you build your brand.

By answering questions and providing help, tips or advice on questions that people have, you can establish yourself as a credible source for information within your niche market, quickly and easily.

Twitter is basically a blog that limits how long your posts can be. Ping your Twitter feed to get it noticed.

You can publish your tweets via an RSS feed. Simply log into your Twitter account, and scroll to the very bottom of your profile page where you will see a **RSS** button available.

You'll want to submit this RSS feed to RSS directories. This gives your Twitter feed more authority by having more links pointing to it.

SQUIDOO

Squidoo is a site that organizes the web based on any imaginable subject. The key here is that you can create a lens on **anything imaginable**. This is where your expertise comes into play. To truly use Squidoo to its fullest capabilities, you must create lenses.

Note lenses, not a lens. Take the information you know and present it in different sections for each individual lens.

You can add in RSS feeds, Blogs, Articles, Del.icio.us$^©$ posts, Youtube Videos, Affiliate Sections relating to your lens, Links to good informative content and much more.

When setting up my lens, I typically include two text based articles and one YouTube video.

To monetize Squidoo properly, you must advertise yourself in every lens you create. Whether you do this by posting an article with a resource box or by posting a link to your blog or website, you must include something about you in every lens.

I recommend creating at least three subject-related lenses.

Link your lenses together to make them easy for your visitors to find. Squidoo advertises your lenses for you to other members of the site which will help with your online visibility.

When formatting your lenses, don't use their affiliate content.

You want to use them to drive traffic to your sites, not your competitors.

Put links throughout your content spread into every different module to make it easy for them to click and follow through to your websites.

HUBPAGES

Hubpages is very similar to Squidoo. Here are the differences:

Their rating system is awesome. It's set between 1 and 100 and you get rated by visitors.

You're only allowed to post 2 links inside of the content of each Hubpage.

You can use huge images on the site and make your hub look amazing.

You can use Flickr photos with ease.

They have a requests feature where you can create hubs that other members are looking for.

The members actually interact with you!

Create multiple hubs and interconnect them by using similar tags.

EASY BLOGGING DOMINATION SYSTEM

Using this system, your blog will become a dynamo attracting customers with next to no effort.

Every time you post, you must ping Blog directories. I've included my Wordpress ping list that will ping for you, but I do it manually to make sure that the sites know I've updated my blog. Use these websites to ping:

www.pingomatic.com

www.ipings.com

Social Bookmark your posts using SocialPoster.com.

The next step is to submit your RSS feed to blog directories.

Find high traffic blogs in your niche. Use your main keyword and use Google's Blog Search to see what others are talking about. Find posts that you can add value to and do it! Another great way to do this is to setup Google Alerts to let you know when someone is discussing something you can add your own spin to.

Be sure to include methods of capturing your visitors and motivate them to come back.

Copy your Autoresponder code into a text module and post it on the top of your sidebar!

Suggest that they subscribe to your RSS feed and put an email capture form in your sidebar.

This should take roughly one hour to submit your feeds and 10 to 15 minutes every time you post.

As time goes on, the links pointing to your blog will compound and give you better rankings with less effort.

CHAPTER 13: PODCASTS

I recommend incorporating Podcasts into your social marketing campaign.

Podcasts are an MP3 file of you talking about anything you can imagine. Once again, these should be informative, entertaining, and valuable. You must then take these podcasts and submit them to Podcast directories. People will load them onto their MP3 players and listen to them at their leisure.

I recommend incorporating podcasts and youtube videos into your blogs to generate more interaction from your visitors.

The competition right now for podcasts is so low that it is literally a wide-open playing field in nearly any niche.

Audacity is great free audio mixing software - http://audacity.sourceforge.net/

You need the lame plug-in for MP3s - http://lame.jthz.com/

Formatting your Podcast is simple with the software above, but you need to make sure it compares to your competition.

Find a Podcast from a name you recognize in your industry. Listen to it! Do your best to mirror the level of professionalism found in the Podcast.

You can get inexpensive intro audio samples here: http://www.audiobag.com

To manage your Podcast, I strongly recommend creating a new Wordpress blog and adding the Podpress© plugin to it. It will add a second RSS feed to your blog automatically that will give you the ability to distribute your podcast to podcast directories and RSS aggregators. It also makes it a breeze to set your podcast up for ITunes and other sites.

CHAPTER 14: SOCIAL NETWORKS

The web has gone social.

You know it, I know it, and the people that came up with Digg™, Twitter™, and Facebook™ definitely know it.

Every single one of these sites can be figured out by doing one simple thing.

Explore their navigation.

That's it.

If there is a way to interact with your prospects, you should.

Simple.

If only it was that easy...

How do you reach them the right way?

How do you advertise without offending?

How do you facilitate positive relationships without sounding and/or looking like a spammer?

The key is to only post valuable content and actually interact with your audience in a way that makes them feel like a part of your community.

Social networking is all about community. If your prospects feel special and you help them with their goals, they're going to enjoy listening to you and interacting with you online.

You can provoke this kind of feeling by giving them things that they can use. Useful websites, ideas, and a feeling of overall community between you and your other prospects will increase interaction and interest with your following.

This is where strategy comes into play. Figure out what your audience wants to hear about from you. Find locations to get updates and information they'll want to see and visit them for a moment or two every day. Find a list of resource sites your prospects will enjoy and bookmark them for later sharing.

Then, share.

Where and how you share these ideas is going to be based upon you and your audience.

You need to communicate in a way that comes easy to you and your prospects can absorb.

Videos, blog posts, articles, audio, etc…
We've covered a lot of these different types of
content previously.

Note: Remember that YouTube, Twitter,
Forums, and other types of sites are all social
networks. *You can and should use the
networking aspects of these sites to increase
your audience.*

Forums are the original social network.
Forums are websites that are set up for people
to have an on-going conversation regarding
their personal experience within the subject of
the forum. Search for your main keywords
with the term "forum" added to it. Be sure to
use both Google and Yahoo to make sure
you're using the highest ranked forums online.
You discuss issues with people in your area of
business.

The marketing part comes in what is called a
signature. In your signature, you are allowed
to post links to your websites.

You are permitted to use only certain things in
your signature, so be sure to read the forum
rules before adding anything to your signature
at all.

Here is how you market yourself on forums:

- Post 4 – 5 (or more) times daily with valuable information immediately upon joining a forum.

- Do not post your signature until 2 to 3 weeks after you join (all of your previous posts will add your signature automatically, so don't worry about having to go and edit any previous posts.

There are two types of code used in signatures to generate a link on a forum:

Html Link: <a href="url">Text to be displayed</a>

Forum code link: [url="url"]Text to be displayed[/url]

158

To market on a forum, you don't market at all. This must sound odd, but it's the honest truth. You give honest and helpful information and you will receive visitors to your website.

Once you fill up the forums in your niche, broaden it. Selling online is something we all do and has hundreds of forums.

Some forums have an area where you can post your services or products. **Do not post to these until you have generated some decent posts.** If you join a forum and head straight for the advertising section, you'll get very bad results. Wait until you add your signature and then post in the advertising area.

Facebook has become the premier social networking website with millions of users looking to connect with other people that enjoy the same things they do. It's also a great way to connect with your customers.

Facebook has taken over the Internet in less time than it took MySpace™ or YouTube. One of the main reasons is its standard level of spam protection. Facebook makes it very difficult for you to simply contact anyone you want. People can't send you messages unless they're connected to you as a friend.

You have to add someone to your friends to be able to talk to them. The nicest part is that they make it easy for you to contact people. I can send one of my videos to all of my friends with just a few clicks.

Even better, once you add your friends in your industry, Facebook makes the growth of your network automatic. When people go through the process of adding friends, Facebook suggests you as a friend to them. I added roughly 200 friends in my industry and now have 4,600 (as of today). Simply add people that you know are connected to your potential customers and let Facebook do the work for you.

Another great way of reaching people is to put on an event. Whether it's a product launch, an actual networking event, or something else entirely, it's very easy to send it to your entire list of friends.

Facebook has its own targeted PPC program that can be used to reach new people. Their membership is growing by thousands per day and you can reach any type of person based on the super targeted nature of the ads.

A really cool way to market anything on Facebook is to create an application and make it viral. Your application can be literally anything you can imagine. Solve one of any type of problem that faces your market and put it out to your friends. The next page must be a "tell your friends" type page that will allow your friends to send it to their friends. This will grow your list through Facebook without you ever having to do anything at all after the original setup of your widget.

I reached out to my friend Mari Smith for some Facebook tips and she gave me two that you should seriously pay attention to:

Facebook as a lead capture source? "You bet!" says renowned Facebook expert, Mari Smith.

One of the first apps to add to your Facebook Fan Page is "FBML" (Facebook Markup Language) – >which allows you to add your own custom content, including an opt-in box. You can add multiple iterations of the FBML app, and try out various lead-capture systems:

ezine signup, giveaway, ask >campaign, etc.
Each opt-in box can appear on a separate tab
with its own unique URL, allowing you to
accurately split test results. For more ways to
market your business on Facebook, pick up a
>copy of Mari's new book Facebook
Marketing: An Hour A Day
http://bit.ly/facebook-mktg

"The most targeted traffic your advertising
dollars can buy," says Facebook expert, Mari
Smith about Facebook ads.

With a quarter million users logging on daily,
Facebook is the number one social >network
in the world and the second most trafficked
site on the web. The amount of data users
willingly share makes Facebook fertile ground
for hyper-targeted ads. For example, you
could take out >an ad that would only be
served to women age 25-35, who are engaged
to be married, who live in San Diego, who are
Justin Bieber fans!

Getting your ad just right is an art and science
and Mari >delves deep into this topic in her
new book, Facebook Marketing: An Hour A
Day – which comes with a series of free online
workshops at http://fanpageworkshop.com

LINKEDIN

LinkedIn® is the top business social network. With over 60 million users, anyone that operates a business should have their profile setup on LinkedIn.

The LinkedIn website is strictly business, point blank.

Spam rules are perfect, yet they make it very easy for you to reach your contacts.

LinkedIn has a status update feature that functions in a similar way to Facebook and Twitter.

Their "Answers" function is very cool and allows you to prove your expertise very easily. You help others and meet new people.

LinkedIn is built for professionals to connect and with definitely help you look more professional in the race to be "The Expert".

MYSPACE

MySpace® is dying in my market.

However your prospects may still be there on a daily basis.

I would like to note that if your niche is in the music industry or connected in any way to it, then give MySpace more than just a look because up and coming musicians use MySpace extensively as a place to post and get music noticed.

There are also niche social networks that cover nearly every interest under the sun.

With social marketing being so different from the standard "in your face" style of driving traffic, be cautious when searching for new networks to use.

Every single one can become a massive time vacuum that keeps you from more important things.

Always watch and test to be sure that your efforts will bring in results.

NON- STANDARD SOCIAL SITES

The term "Wiki" sounds like some foreign weapon, but what it truly does is give a social network that provides information.

To see the largest Wiki in action, check out http://wikipedia.org.

The main idea behind Wikis is to provide a platform that can be openly edited by anyone that visits its pages.

Through "crowd sourcing", the thought was that relevant information would help tons of people.

You can build links and traffic through Wikis by adding details about what you products do to their sites.

My favorite "social time saver" is ping.fm, it allows you to post your updates to dozens of social networking sites at once.

They also have mobile applications for Iphone® and Android® phones that make it very easy to post from wherever your day may take you.

There are social networks you can find and join, hundreds of them in fact.

Many of them will be based on specific ideas like dog lovers, parents, baby boomers, etc...

Their member base may not be as large as Facebook, but if you sell in that market, nearly all members are a potential customer for your niche.

Contribute, add value, and snag new customers from these sites!

CHAPTER 15:   PRESS RELEASE MARKETING

Submitting press releases gets you exposure on sites like Google and Yahoo News©, along with many other websites related to your business.

Press releases generate targeted traffic and then some.

What do you think would happen if you were featured in a large magazine or on a television interview? You would get a ton of traffic to your website.

Press releases must be formatted for the press and not as an advertisement.

You must tease the reader and hope that a valuable member of the press will want to know more about you.

You can submit as many press releases as you want for any relevant event.

Some examples of reasons to post a press release are:

- A new website

- A special sale

- A promotion within your company (New CEO)

- A new product

- A special event

- A strategic partnership

- An award received

You can use free distribution sites but the best premium press release site is www.prweb.com.

Here is the basic format for a decent press release to promote a website:

FOR IMMEDIATE RELEASE

11/21/2006

The headline should capture your readers' attention and include your best keyword.

- The summary should arouse curiosity in the reader to read the rest of your press release. It is very important to make it interesting and not dull.

City, State - date - Intro statement

The intro statement should read like a story and begin to answer who, what, when, why, and how. DON'T pitch your website here. At the first "whiff" of a pitch people are going to be turned off from your release.

Instead of pitching you should continue to "tease" the reader into wanting to find out more information by visiting your website.

You can start with a quotation or a statement that gets attention. It should speak to a hot-button that the media can quickly begin to picture for a story... or give other readers an intriguing story so they want to learn more about you on your website.

Now expand on your intro statement.

You can include quotes or statements here to add news value. Statistics are also useful, but should be simple and to the point.

A Tip or Topic List

Examples For A Tip List Include:

- 7 Quick and Easy Ways To Lose Weight

- 10 Ways To Stay Hydrated During Hot Days

- 5 Ways To Have Your Kids Stay Safe This Halloween

Examples For A Topic List Include:

- There are 3 different reasons people fail with diets

- There are 10 causes of tooth decay

- There are 7 reasons parents fail when raising their child

For the topics you would expound on each one and tell what you are.

These topic and tip lists should give a taste of what else you have to offer. Make it short and sweet with the purpose of leading the reader to want to contact you or visit your website and buy.

Summary or Concluding Sentence

Mention your website here, explain how it will help the public.

Example: Dr. John Smart studies the effects of tooth decay and publishes his results in a free monthly electronic magazine entitled, "Tooth Decay Chronicles."

Contact (your name) for more insights into this topic. Direct line: (555) 555-5555 Email: Other helpful information regarding the can be found at: http://www.YourWebsite.com.

Important Note: It is important to include the website URL that you want ranked at least 1 time in your body and at least twice for the entire release.

For More Information Contact:

Your Contact Information

Your Audience

Write to your audience with a press release. If you want media exposure and are pretty sure you can get it, go for it! If you are happy with pulling in a few new customers, then customize your release to speak directly to them.

Don't be shy! If you have a story that would fit your local news, pick up the phone and find out where to send your release for their consideration. If you have contacts at a local TV station, use them.

PRWeb is the premier press release distribution service. To get amazing exposure, you can spend a few hundred dollars and be on their front page. You will get thousands of visitors for this. When deciding whether to upgrade to a high cost distribution, you must figure out how large your audience is.

If your products or services apply to the masses, pay for the upgrade!

CHAPTER 16: SOFTWARE MARKETING

Creating a useful tool for your customers and prospects gives you the ability to help them and help yourself. It also gives you the ability to get backlinks from massively popular download sites.

The first thing that has to be done is you have to have software to give away or sell. To get the most from download websites, you're going to want to have a free version that you can distribute.

Figuring out what your software is going to do is always going to be based on your prospects and the problems your products provide. When I sold mattresses, I put together a plan for a software program that tracked the sleep a person would get each night. The plan was to remind them periodically of the importance of their sleep surface and how it relates to the quality of the sleep we get. While the software didn't get made, it turned into a software program used to find keywords we're already getting traffic for that we may not be aware of called Trakr. You'll find out more about that later on in the book.

Finding a programmer can be time consuming and very difficult. Depending on the intensity of the work needed to create your software, you could have it done in days or it could take months to complete.

Reliable programmers are really hard to find. You could use sites like Elance©, Guru.com©, or VWorker.com©, but you have to dig through a lot of garbage people to find someone worth working with. To find my programmers, I usually turn to friends. In fact, my current main programmer came from a recommendation from a close business friend and we've been working together for years now.

Tip: Give a tiny project to programmers you don't know to test how they react to timelines and if they provide you with a product that meets your specifications.

The easiest way to layout your design vision for your software is to use a graphics program to give what's called a "wire frame" to your programmer. The wire frame should give a visual representation of what your software is going to look like. Once you have that part done, you need to create a specification sheet that gives extreme detail about what your software is going to do for the user. Be sure to cover things like registration systems, colors, functions (usually it's best to give a step by step set of directions for this part), ad space and where you'll want it, what your free version needs to do and any other important details.

If and when, you find a good programmer, do whatever you can to keep them and keep them happy. It's a challenging process and you'll want to work with good people often once you find them.

The next step is to create what's called a pad file. A pad file tells download sites all about your software and makes it very easier to distribute your software to those sites.

Upload your pad file and your software to a location on your website.

Next, submit the pad file location to download websites.

This gives you additional backlinks and will raise your rankings in Google.

CHAPTER 17: VIRAL MARKETING

Viral Marketing is not what most people think it is.

Most of the time, the best viral marketing uses strategies we've already discussed: videos, articles, blogs, press releases, etc…

Viral marketing is based upon something simple: Providing great content or something worth talking about in a way that your audience finds it. If they find it, they're going to spread it around, because it's just that good.

Those consumed with SEO will try to manipulate their way to viral exposure and usually end up wasting their energies. If they simply created really good content, it would all happen naturally. While I'm known for my SEO prowess, my videos that have gone viral have done so all on their own, without any manipulation. The reason is that the content is great and helps people.

My videos have surpassed others for one main reason: They aren't a veiled pitch (which is exactly what nearly all of my competition is).

By not mentioning my products, I created a viral growth that most people would happily pay for…

The secret was to not focus on the results. My initial goal was to become an authority for the topic of "Affiliate Marketing" in the eyes of my market and it was at a time when YouTube was emerging as a major force, before Google bought it.

I created a series of three videos with nothing, but content.

One of them took off and bypassed the others. It was published in a major affiliate marketing forum and 3 years later it is still ranked well and has around 80,000 views.

There is no other video for the term "affiliate marketing" that has anywhere near that amount of views.

I've done zero link building to the video (which is how you get a video to increase in rankings, just like anything else).

The growth was 100% natural and happened all on its own.

Here's the formula, so you can replicate it:

- Give the best content you can.

- Don't mention a website at all.

- If you want to link to a website, put it in your description as the first thing they see if they look.

- Be sure to mention it on social media sites you have built a presence on.

- Watch as it soars.

It's really, truly and honestly that simple.

You can deliver your message any way you want, it can be done through mobile applications, free Ebooks, articles, etc...

They method of delivery is nowhere near as important as the content inside of it.

Recently, I tested a strategy where I gave away software that I should have charged for. My closest competitor charges around $80 per year for a similar product.

By giving it away, it caught on very quickly and created a bunch of leads for me without any further work. It truly went viral.

The secret was that anyone that registered the software automatically was placed into my email list.

Every download meant more leads for me.

Now, there is another type of viral marketing that I want to expose to you, because if you do it right, it leads to massive exposure that costs you next to nothing.

This type of viral marketing is based upon providing a bribe to get someone to help you spread your message.

By doing this, you give someone a reason to help you by helping them in some way, shape, or form.

If done right, it ends up helping you both.

We can call this "forced viral marketing".

This is facilitated through scripts that track what they do.

There are hundreds of different ways to do it from tracking when someone tweets or posts to Facebook to tracking when they use a "tell a friend" script.

Tell a friend scripts are scripts hosted on your site that will make it easy for those that visit your site to fill out a simple form and email their friends a recommendation that they check out this cool free tool, report, or video that you've created.

In return, you give them an additional piece of content for spreading the word. If you frame it properly, they'll be thrilled to share it with their friends and you get to feel good that you're helping them.

Another thing you should do is make it easy for others to share your content with others. Linking to social sites like Twitter, Facebook, LinkedIn, MySpace, and social bookmarking sites is easy to do and mandatory if you want your ideas spread around by your audience.

The easiest way to implement this is by using a social plugin on a WordPress blog.

I use sociable, but there are dozens of others. Also, be sure to use the "Facebook Like" plugin.

Yet, that still only barely covers viral marketing.

Contests are a great way to grab the attention of your marketplace. Give something away and post the contest info to contest sites. Nice and easy.

Free software, like what I discussed before, can go very viral by simply putting them on free download sites.

First, you have to create a pad file (search Google for "pad file creator", they're available for free). Then, you submit that file to the sites and they help people find you.

Just remember to make your content amazing. If it is, you're going to get viral action on the stuff you put out.

CHAPTER 18: PARTNERING

AFFILIATE PROGRAMS

Affiliate programs can truly take your business to the next level.

What you do is offer to pay your affiliates if they refer a customer that ends up buying from you. The percentage you pay will be anything from 5 – 75% and it is completely up to you. As I'm sure you've figured out, the more you pay out, the more affiliates you will have.

Setting up your affiliate program must include some crucial pieces:

- Software to manage your affiliates

- Tracking of the amount owed to your affiliates

- Advertising materials (emails, banners, images, AdWords ads, viral Ebooks, and anything else you can think of that they might need to sell for you)

How you set up your affiliate program depends on your products.

Here are digital product programs:

www.clickbank.com

www.2co.com

www.paydotcom.com

Affiliate programs for physical products can be found on these websites:

www.cj.com

www.linkshare.com

There is a very thin line between promoting products and becoming a spammer in the eyes of your subscribers and customers.

Don't get greedy and feel free to be picky when it comes to promoting the products of others.

As an affiliate, you must provide value to your customers at all times.

If you do that, they will buy what you recommend.

Once your affiliate program is setup, be sure to make it findable for affiliates! Submit your affiliate program to affiliate directories ASAP!

Implement affiliate and joint venture deals by contacting the owner of a complimentary site to set up a cross-selling type relationship.

This means that if any of his customers ask where they should buy their next IPod, the owner will refer them to you. This also means that you have to do the same. In exchange for this, you give each other a percentage of the money earned from your relationship.

Developing relationships will do amazing things for your business.

You must set up a way of tracking joint venture efforts to ensure you get paid. There are many ways of tracking these efforts, but the easiest way is to set up a specific page for that customer for them to send their customers to. That way you can track which orders come from them. If you have a shopping cart with numerous products, most have affiliate modifications that can be applied that will tell you when an affiliate makes a sale and how much you owe them.

Remember that you don't have to have an affiliate program in place to do a joint venture. If you have a mailing list and your potential partner does too, check to see if they would be willing to send a recommendation to their list without a link to get paid. As long as you're willing to do the same, this works to benefit both of you.

Many potential partners will be willing to do something special for you to promote their products. You should be willing to do the same using teleseminars, webinars, custom emails, etc...

Over deliver to a JV partner and they may just refer you to their friends and other people that they may know in your niche.

Also, a JV doesn't just have to be to promote each other's products. It could be working together to create one!

Digital information products are easily created between two or more people that have knowledge on a subject!

Secret Tip: Always make sure that every folder of your website has an index page. Otherwise thieves can find and take any files easily.

This is an acceptable practice for **affiliate marketing**, as well.

Finding affiliates used to be quite the difficult task.

Clickbank hides affiliates behind their user names and makes it nearly impossible to figure out who they are (search Google for their user id and you might get lucky).

Private affiliate programs don't reveal users either.

Here are some sites you can use to find new potential affiliates for your products:

Social Networks:

Use the search function on Social Networks to search for products that are similar to yours.

You will find others that are promoting those (hopefully) inferior products and will be able to approach them with your product.

Be sure to build a real relationship by adding them as a friend and researching them a bit.

Squidoo:

With the nearly automatic Google ranking of Squidoo lenses, every product launch leads to 20 new lenses based on a specific product. Search for recent products on Squidoo and contact those that create good lenses based on those products.

Video Sites:

Google's Universal Search has made video even more important when it comes to affiliate marketing. Do a Video Search using the name of recently launched products and you will find potential affiliates.

The Best Part:

Affiliates using the methods above are on top of their game! They are using what works and this will help you earn more money in less time.

The three methods above are an extremely small piece of what you could be doing. Sites like Hubpages™, MyBlogLog™, and many others can all be used exactly like the sites above.

How To Contact Them:

One new affiliate could earn you thousands of dollars in income. Approaching them properly is the most important thing you could do to gain their trust.

Nobody wants to promote a product they haven't seen. Offer them a copy of yours. The worst case is that you just lost a potential sale. The best case is that they will get you dozens!

Research them as thoroughly as you can. By searching for their ID in Google, you could find the rest of their memberships and learn all kinds of details about them. It's a necessity that you personalize your contact with them. Talk about your shared interests, families, and business ideas. It's OK to use a template message for all affiliates, but make sure you leave room for personalization.

Always be sure to offer to return the favor with their products. If they don't have products, offer bonuses for their list or purchasers.

Last, But Not Least:

Be sure that their tactics are ones that actually work. Sign up for their newsletters and watch their messages that they send. Read their blog posts. Check out their web pages. Don't waste time on affiliates that won't sell much, you'll find that most of those will contact you on their own.

Advertising offers on "thank you pages" sends a new customer (immediately after a sale) to a friend or through an affiliate link. This is normally done on a post purchase page where product is delivered or shipping instructions will be placed. By offering someone that just paid you a product that is useful in addition to what they just purchased, the odds of them buying that product go way up. Offer integration pieces to your affiliates and exchange ads with those that have complementary products to what you sell.

One of the biggest challenges with having an affiliate program is knowing how to motivate your affiliates to get out there and bring in sales for you.

I reached out to my buddy, Anik Singal and asked him to put something together that shows you how to get your affiliates to work for you:

5 POWER-PACKED METHODS FOR MAXIMIZING PARTNER PROMOTIONS

By Anik Singal, Founder and CEO, Lurn, Inc.

Once you've launched your affiliate business and have offers to promote, you are going to want to reach out to other marketers in your niche and promote to their customer lists. Of course you will have to share the revenue with those promoters in exchange for access to their audience, but it's worth it. Simply put, if you have a good offer but are not promoting through others in your space, you are absorbing the cost of lost opportunity. But if you split the revenue to connect with more customers sooner, you are gaining sales you would probably not have gotten anyway. Also, once those customers convert, you will have the best prospects' contact info for direct promotions later. So, there is a lot of immediate and ongoing benefit to promoting your offers through partners.

But before we get to the tips, how do you get partners? Well, these are the people in your topical space doing what you do who may not have a similar offer. If you are an affiliate marketing expert offering software to do 'content spinning,' you might consider partner with marketers offering on-site SEO marketing tools. This is an example of two marketers with a very different focus but an audience with the same need: to gain website traffic.

Now, on to the fun stuff. We've done some of the best partner promotions in the business. We've given away cars, computers, and lots of other cool toys. But we're not haphazardly buying access to lists. We are very intentional in our work to build relationships and reward our joint venture partners.

Here are the things we do that have been the most important for our success in working with partners:

Let 'Em Know What's Coming

Once you've built a network of people serving similar audiences, stay in touch. Be careful not to give away your ideas, but share with them what's coming so they can plan ahead. Good promoters keep an editorial calendar for their partner promotions and their own promotions. You need to let them know when you will launch your offers or products so they can schedule for it. Relationships are a major key in most businesses, but they are absolutely critical in joint venture promotions. Fortunately, potential partners are probably going to have promotions they need help with too. That mutual need creates a natural incentive to work together since you can help them with their launches. Build your network, build your ties to others, and coordinate.

Keep Score

People like to win. They like to be at the top of a ranking. If you are doing a big launch, let your affiliates know that others will be promoting and make it a friendly competition. Plan ahead to use some revenue for fun prizes or cash bonuses. Give away the latest and hottest prizes like in iPad, a Mac Book Pro, or a satellite radio. Create a simple leader board and let everyone see where they are in the running. As long as you are tracking performance through each partner, you can easily update the score daily.

Affiliate partners will compete for better prize packages thus driving more sales for you.

Exclusive Bonuses

Develop exclusive bonus items to be included for each major partner. These are free items that go with your offer to the partner's customers. An example is that if you are offering a new 'content spinner' software, you could include a bonus such a "Guide to Evaluating the Hottest Niches." The guide could be used only in promotions to a particular partner's list. This bonus strategy leverages the unique connection the audience has to the partner.

Warm It Up

Have the partner help you warm up their audience.

Consider these two approaches:

1) Hey everyone, check out this thing from a friend of mine, versus,

2) Hey everyone, I am going to interview Bob Smith tonight on his groundbreaking new.... Obviously, the content of the second version is going to be more familiar to the partners' audience. It can be simply an introduction and a reading of 2-3 questions to have the speaker

cover. If you are doing webinars or other free content to promote your launch, having the affiliate partner warm up the audience by being personally involved will greatly increase the performance of the promotion.

Follow It Up

Not all audience members are going to get the first message. For your most valuable partners, consider 2-3 communications to get the most out of every opportunity. This one is hard because you are asking a lot from the partner. So you may need to consider a graduated performance scale to make the extra access worth their time and permission. A good model that does not require too much work is to send multiple emails leading up to an "interview" webinar. This gives adequate time for people to get the message and then one time that you have to schedule and speak. But then, follow up on the webinar with a link to the recording for everyone. This little step of offering the webinar after the fact can add another 10-30%. Sometimes people can't attend live because it simply does not fit their schedule. Warming it up and following it up are the best ways to make the most of every effort.

Building a successful network of promotion partners is a "flywheel" activity. Once you have the network, you have the ability to do one solid, effective promotion. The more of those you do, the more partners you can attract. Sharing previous (and successful) results will be very compelling when approaching new partners. So, start somewhere that you think you will get good results such as with a partner with a very similar audience profile. Then build on your success and grow the momentum with each offer and promotion.

Happy marketing!

Also, if you want to jump-start your career as an affiliate marketer, check out this video with Anik discussing exactly how to do that:

http://blog.affiliateclassroom.com/yourbusiness

JOINT VENTURE MAGIC

Joint Ventures are one of the main factors in my personal success. Of course, it hasn't hurt my training products actually do what the sales pages claim.

Creating joint ventures is so much more than finding a simple affiliate. You have to treat joint venture relationships as real friendships with the necessary trust you would give a true friend. This puts you both at risk, but is worth it if all goes well.

The single best way to joint venture with people is to meet them face to face. This can be done through seminars, business meetings, trade shows, local organizations and many other methods. My personal success comes straight from Internet marketing seminars. In fact, I just put on my first seminar last weekend!

Meeting face to face give you the chance to base your opinion of someone on how you feel in their presence. Most of us have that inner radar that will make us uncomfortable around crappy people. Shaking their hand allows you to get past that issue (as long as they don't creep you out).

Once you meet a potential JV partner, you must offer value. This value can be anything from an extra percentage of sales to reciprocation to special bonuses just for them. There are no limits on what you can do to provide value to your partners. Treat them like gold and they will come back for your next product!

There are dozens of other ways to setup joint ventures. Here are some ideas:

- Combine one of your products with one of your associates to create a complimentary deal for both of your groups of customers and split the revenue.

- Facilitate joint ventures between other companies and take a small percentage of the sales.

- Offering a special discount in a private promotion that you allow one of your affiliates offer at a time.

Joint Ventures are a deeper arrangement or relationship than the standard affiliate arrangement and should be handled as though you're dealing with friends.

Of course, you'll still want to have documentation in place to protect both parties involved, but keep it as informal as you can to ensure that everyone involved is excited about the arrangement.

I recently met a "JV Ninja" named Sohail Kahn. When I reached out and asked him to give something that would help you better "get" joint ventures, he sent me this:

HOW TO WRITE A KILLER JOINT VENTURE PROPOSAL

Below are the **key steps** in writing a killer JV proposal:

1. **Use a captivating headline** or opening sentence that offers your JV partner a great benefit, picques their curiosity and compels them to read your whole letter. If the headline and/or opening sentence is targeted and good enough, they will read the next one etc. If any part of your offer is not compelling enough, they won't read the rest and you will lose them.

2. **Introduce and present yourself** in such a way as to show them that you are serious, professional, and trustworthy.

3. **Make sure you are very clear** as to what you want to do. Specify all the ideas and plans that you have in mind. Being vague will not work in your favor as people are busy.

4. **Make your prospects feel unique** and special.

5. **Make your offer hard to resist.**
Remember that you have to sell your joint
venture to your potential partner. Write it like a
sales letter and do not hard-sell them. Pull
them into your offer, incite them to accept your
offer.

6. **Explain who you are,** how long you have
been in business, what your product or service
is like, how many people you have in your
customer list, how responsive they are, your
website URL, your conversion rate and any
other info that you believe would be of interest
to the other party for them to make an
educated decision.

7. **Make it look simple.** Keep it organized
and logical.

8. **Be sure to make it personal.** This is
extremely important. Always us their name.
Remember use your Alexa and Whois online
searches and use that information to write
your proposal. When you send them an email
or a letter with all that hard to find information
you will probably capture their attention and
you will look more professional.

9. **When mailing your proposal,** you have to know about the A, B and C piles. When people receive mail, they always sort it out – they put everything that's personal (or that looks personal) in one pile (the 'A' pile). Then they take what looks more or less important and put it in the 'B' pile to be opened later. The rest (the 'C' pile also known as junk mail) is simply thrown away. So your goal is to be in the 'A' pile – using the FedEx approach as discussed earlier will almost guarantee your proposal gets the right attention.

10. **Be sure to make your JV proposal standout** from the rest. If people are used to splitting profits 50/50 in a joint venture (remember you make your commission on the overall result of the joint venture deal), why not offer more on the first number of sales or even better give them ALL the profit if you have greater high ticket back-end profits you can make. This way the partner will push your product.

11. **Put the decision makers name in the headline.** The following email subject line has gotten a VERY high response rate for me: Dear Name, I want to work with you…

12. **Always offer a guarantee** and take away any risk if you can do it. Try the following in your body copy: "I want to send you my _____ so you can review it. I am just asking for a few minutes of your time. This is what I mean: spend a few moments to skim over my _____ and if it doesn't live up to your expectations, let me know and I will immediately pay you _____ for your efforts".

13. **Put yourself in your prospect's shoes** when writing your letter.

14. **Be sure to write your proposal carefully** and to proofread it several times before firing it off. An excellent way to find mistakes in whatever you write is to read it out loud. Have someone else proofread it also.

15. **If you have any testimonials from other people/businesses** that you've joint ventured with, use them. A strong testimonial that gives figures and results is better. If you can prove that you're honest, hardworking and that you've been very successful in the past it's going to be a big plus.

16. **Be sure to let them know that you are familiar with their business.** If you are subscribed to their e-zine or newsletter, say it. If you've bought from them (which I advise you do to see their buying cycle) and like their product/service, say so but only if you are 100% sincere.

17. **If you partnered with people in their industry, say so.** It gives and instant boost to your credibility. They'll think: "OK, if he/she worked with _____ and _____, he/she must be good or have a viable business proposition. This is called 'Social Proof' and is very powerful.

18. **Give them the impression that they'll get a lot more** out of the arrangement than you will.

19. **Put your proposal in bulleted format** and write short paragraphs, It's easier on the eyes and is more liable to be completely read than a big block of text.

20. **Just like in a well crafted sales letter** always use your prospect's first name often and talk to them not at them.

21. **At the end of the letter, tell them what to do and tell them to do it NOW.** If you have deadlines coming up tell them. If not, they may have a tendency to put it off and you'll lose the deal.

22. **Always use some P.S.'s** because they are always read. Some people read the P.S.'s first right after the headline. This is your second headline you use to stress the urgency of the situation or the exclusivity.

To claim your free "Joint Venture Millionaire" DVD that reveals all of Sohail's 6 and 7 figure JV secrets go to:

http://www.freejointventuredvd.com

CHAPTER 19: MOBILE MARKETING

Reaching the cell phones of those you have no relationship with can only be done via paid advertising.

Google's Adwords program now has a specific mobile marketing program that you can target. Outside of them, there are other mobile advertising networks popping up every few days. Do a Google search for "mobile advertising network" to find them. When you do, start small and test the effectiveness of your ads before diving into this type of advertising head first.

Building a list of cell phone numbers isn't as easy as building a standard email list.

People are very protective of their cell numbers due to the fact that most people never leave home without them.

If you setup a special mobile autoresponder with tips or coupons, you may be able to get your prospects to provide their numbers, always test to see what gets the best response from your people.

Iphone and Android applications are another way to reach people on their cell phones. Provide tips, advice, or other cool functions via a mobile application and you'll be able to advertise whatever you want inside your application.

Check out http://appmakr.com for iphone applications and http://isites.us for iphone and android applications.

Both of these services use RSS feeds to add content into your applications.

Remember that nearly all marketing is now mobile marketing with the popularity of the Iphone and, now, Android cell phones. Do everything in your power to be sure that those that visit your sites on their phones are able to experience your entire sales process as well as those at a computer.

HTML5 allows you to create pages that will show your videos to mobile phones with ease. Here is a quick and dirty guide on how to create a simple flow that will identlfy users of apple products and forward them to a page that is friendly to whatever they're using (ipod, iphone, or ipad).

Step 1: The first step is to put this code into your current page at the very beginning of the body of the page (right after the <body> tag):

```
<script type="text/javascript">

if ((navigator.userAgent.indexOf('iPhone') != -1) || (navigator.userAgent.indexOf('iPod') != -1) ||

(navigator.userAgent.indexOf('iPad') != -1)) {

document.location = "IPOD PAGE URL GOES HERE";

}

</script>
```

What this code does is it tells the page to send iPhone, iPod, and iPad users to the page

we're going to format to work with their system.

I had some issues with this code on my page. Be sure to test it thoroughly in multiple

Internet browsers to be sure your content displays properly. If it doesn't, play around with the location of the code until it works.

Step 2: Reformat your video. You need your video to either be in .m4v format or mp4

encoded with the h.264 codec. Most video editors in their newest versions support both of these formats. Camtasia 7 automatically outputs .MP4 videos in the h.264 format and has .M4V built in, too. Out of all the software that I use for video, Camtasia 7 is the easiest way to set this up and format your videos properly without too much effort.

Step 3: Create your iPod friendly page. This part will require some playing around and a lot of testing in multiple browsers. I strongly recommend installing Firefox, Internet Explorer, Chrome, and Safari to be able to test your pages across all 4 browsers.

There are tons of options when it comes to new code with your videos. However, most of them are unnecessary if you can get the code in Step 1 to work. The h.264 codec is playable as flash, so your flash based video on a standard browser should play just fine automatically in all browsers.

The HTML5 page forwarding in step 1 will forward Apple product owners to the page that is formatted for their systems.

This is the code that I recommend using in your page:

<center><video src="**VIDEO SOURCE URL GOES HERE**" width="320 height="320

autobuffer controls>

<div class="fallback">

<p>You must have an HTML5 capable browser to view this video</p>

</div>

</video></center>

You're going to need to test this page on an Apple portable device and it's best that you own one. The cheapest option out there is an iPod touch, however, I guarantee you have a buddy with an iPhone. Have them over and check your page on their device to be sure it's properly formatted.

This is going to require a lot of testing on your part to be sure that it works properly.

HTML5 is very much a work in progress and there are a lot of different ways to set this up. One way has you putting code in a way that it will attempt to load the video in multiple formats and that will work just fine.

There are dozens of tutorials out there that claim to tell you "the right way" to do this. They're all right in some form, so feel free to play with it. Do a Google search for "html5 tutorial" and you'll find a bunch of different ways to implement it on your websites.

The reason I implemented this the way I did is because it was best for sale conversion. The instant shift to a special page for those that use an iPod or similar device didn't interrupt the sales process much, so it works for my needs.

The key isn't to do it the way I did. The key is to simply do it.

CHAPTER 20: INSTANT PUSH BUTTON TRAFFIC

Consider this: You push a button and become a traffic director.

That is what an email list is.

If you are able to contact your customers directly in their email, you can send them anywhere you want.

The most obvious place to direct them is to sites where they can buy from you, but there are other options you need to consider.

If the only messages you send equate to "buy this", your prospects will stop reading what you send them eventually.

You must provide a reason for them to want to read what you're sending them.

The easiest "reason" is to provide value related to what you sell.

Whether it's a content filled newsletter that goes out every week or a monthly report, be sure to give them a reason to stick around and look forward to the emails you send out. People will stick around for awhile if you send out offers, but they'll stick longer if you give them a good reason to.

Sign Up Psychology

Think about what goes through *your* mind before you enter in your name and email address into someone else's subscriber box. We've all done it, but most of it has been totally unconscious.

If you start to tune into your thoughts and feelings before you subscribe or buy you will notice that it always comes down to one thing.

WHAT'S IN IT FOR ME?

Responsive lists are ones that give a "targeted prospect" an irresistible incentive to subscribe. In fact, you have to sell the person on **why they should subscribe to your list** rather than any one of the millions of other lists.

The key is to NOT make your list for everyone. That's right. Read that again.

If your list is for everyone, your list is for no one.

You may be thinking that you want as many subscribers as possible. But if you get a bunch of subscribers that don't care about your offer and don't like you, you are not benefiting from having them on your list. What you want to do is make your stated benefits be targeted toward a certain group of people.

For example, people interested in building computers would love an ezine (digital newsletter) that shows them how to boost computer performance. People only interested in the sport of golf are not going to be signing up for lists that show them how to improve their batting average.

Now there are a few different ways to capture names which we will get into in a second. Regardless of how you get the list, you always want to have some kind of clear visible opt-in box on your website that clearly states the exact benefit someone will get from becoming one of your "valued subscribers".

Benefits that Matter

Not all benefits are created equal.

It's important to say that whatever you decide to do online you should be passionate about. If you are not passionate about your business and your website you will not put your heart into your business and it will eventually fail.

That being said...

Before you begin to even setup your list the first thing you should do is research your target market to get a feel for what people are REALLY looking for.

There are a couple tools you can use to improve your market intelligence. This may not be the sexiest part of the job but it's probably the most important part. If you don't know what people want, how can you give it to them? You can always guess, but do you think the top list-builders are guessing?

Quantcast.com gives you insight into the audience of a website (yours or someone else's). The value in that is being able to cater your language to your specific market. You'll be able to focus on things that specifically resonate with your prospects.

Forums in your niche can be very helpful, too. Simply search Google for your main keywords, plus the word "forum" or "discussion group". Be sure to look for complaints and questions from your potential customers then you are empowered to solve their problems!

Once you really know what your market wants it's time to give it to them. Don't wait and don't procrastinate!

There are a few ways to present your benefits to visitors that come to your site.

1 A free Gift – people love free stuff, especially if you put a price on it.

2 A multiple part free ecourse

3 Ongoing training and tips

4 A special discount

5 A membership- people love to be part of a group or association that they can relate to.

6 The ability to ask questions

7 Interviews with experts

So...now that you've sold your prospects on the benefits it's time to polarize them and deliver on your promise. The first thing to keep in mind is that everyone has a different style of teaching, communicating and relaying information.

Once they sign up, it's a great time to offer them something to purchase. It shouldn't be a huge leap of faith or high cost product, unless that's the only thing you sell. Focus on giving something very special and let them know that it's "they're the type of person you want to work with".

E-courses should be delivered over a short period of time to train your list members to open your emails. With aweber, use the "follow up" feature *(goes out to every member at your specified intervals)* and space your messages properly. They are automatically set at 4 days apart. You should actually send the messages daily or every other day to get them used to hearing from you. "Broadcasts" are one time messages that will go out only to current members of your list. If you plan on promoting products to your list, be sure to start during your e-course. Otherwise, your members will get upset when the promos start rolling in.

Ongoing training and tips should be a part of your messages, even if they are blatant promotions. Always be teaching something to show your expertise and ensure that your members see you as the "go-to person" in your niche. If you educate your list members on why what you are promoting is important and how it will improve their lives or income, they won't be turned off by your recommendations **(promotions)**. Experts sell products, plain and simple.

Discounts are simple enough to show, but be aware that it's easier to sell people over time. In research it's shown that people normally need to see a product 7 times before investing in it. So before you try doing a hundred sales a month, make sure your message and product benefits are being communicated from every angle. If you start running discounts and sales on your own products now stop, your message gets watered down and the prospect has no immediate reason to buy because they know next week you'll just have another sale.

A **free membership program** is an outstanding way to interact with people. Provide a value that people will see as a solution. Offer an upsell to a platinum or special membership that offers more.

Being able to "ask the expert" is very attractive to someone that is trying to learn how to do something online. This can be done through a forum and is a great way to distribute your work, time and expertise. It's extremely effective if done properly. Be sure to check in on your forum often.

Don't get upset if you have any people that leave, you actually want them to. If you don't have anyone unsubscribing it means you're too plain for everyone to get noticed. Just deliver the benefits you promised in your own unique way. If you try to impersonate another person's style you will do terrible because your message and "online personality" won't flow properly.

It never hurts to implement ideas you learned in business or marketing but continue to be yourself, **it's often the only thing that sets you apart from others and can be the difference between someone staying on your list or going to someone else's similar list**.

To Squeeze or Not to Squeeze

A squeeze page is a simple page that provokes visitors to sign up to your email list in exchange for information regarding the subject they want more information on.

There's a reason why marketers use squeeze pages. It's because they quickly convert browsers into subscribers while delivering value through follow-up. It also helps cut back on the chance of losing the prospect forever.

If you think about it a squeeze page sells a visitor on the promise of providing the benefits stated in bullet points on the site. Whether or not that promise is fulfilled is your job. Now, some visitors may be turned off by the squeeze page and you will lose them but statistically speaking it will help to build your list much faster. And if the benefits are enticing and the prospects really are hot for your product they will subscribe.

The thing to test is whether or not you are losing more subscribers with or without it. You will probably find that you are losing more without using a squeeze page.

IF YOU DON'T USE A SQUEEZE PAGE

You should always have an easy to see opt in subscriber box with as few boxes as possible. I've even seen some websites ask for your email and when you hit subscribe they take you to a second page that has a whole bunch of forms for you to finish filling out.

This is a highly effective technique if you need to gather extensive information. Because your prospect has already invested in a small amount of time, they are more likely to fill out their remaining details.

Just make sure you never ask for more information than you absolutely need.

The best place to put an opt-in box is obviously the top of the page. In testing, the best place to put your opt-in box is on the top right. I have seen them in the header and in the sidebars.

As long as it's plainly visible and a short, enticing offer of benefits is clearly stated this will allow you to capture more names than if you had none.

Put your opt-in box on as many places as you have access to: MySpace profiles and other social networks, your blogs, your websites and anywhere else you can think.

The more chances you give a person to sign up for your list, the higher the odds that they will do just that.

SECRET WEAPONS

Exit popups have become extremely popular. They will only show up when your visitor is about to leave your page.

It will irritate some, but the benefit of using one will far outweigh the negative aspect of it, as long as you don't make them fight through 5 of them to leave your website.

This technique is completely non-invasive as the customer doesn't see anything while browsing your site. If they leave or close the window without buying you would normally lose them forever. So why not give them an "in-your-face" message after they've left your site that gives them a break down of the best benefits they will be missing out on if they don't subscribe?

There are some really cool types of exit popups that grab the attention of your reader and force them to take an extra step before leaving. It's an awesome opportunity to get a "last chance" offer in front of your visitors.

Even if the conversions are low, over time you will pull in hundreds if not thousands of more subscribers you would have otherwise lost.

This is the perfect method to capture a prospect that you would have lost otherwise.

Always keep in mind that tactics like exit the popup will anger some people that visit your sites.

Keep it simple and don't force them to go through 5 screens and popups just to leave.

**Hot Tip! A new version of a popup ad that is far less intrusive has been shown to double, triple, or even quadruple the amount of people that sign up for your list. They are called footer slideup ads. By being less intrusive, people are much more likely to sign up for your list with a positive attitude.

SETTING UP YOUR AUTORESPONDER

The perfect plan behind building your list is too have it run on its own as much as possible.

Most people plug in a few autoresponder messages and get bogged down by busy work and forget about it.

Make a commitment to yourself to plug in "evergreen" information and do at least one every other day.

If you sent out your messages spaced 3 days apart, then after about 4 months you would have an autoresponder that contacts your customers for a full year without you ever writing another email again.

If you have golf clubs list and a golf swing tutorial site. They would be more likely to work together.

So use only what you need but keep in mind that the more "segmented" your list is- the faster your subscribers will hit the buy button when you send a highly targeted list related promotion.

Every new subscriber who opts in will get the benefit of your one time work for a full year. The key here is not to get trigger happy and go on a message writing rampage.

Take your time and write down ideas as they come and write messages that provide a mix of content and promotion in your emails.

I see far too many list owners sending prewritten messages to their list simply to promote affiliate programs.

Eventually people will catch on and unsubscribe.

That doesn't show any skill or expertise, it simply establishes you as an ad whore. Write original and unique content, subscribers will always flock to well written useful content with originality.

Gain their trust, interact, and they will pay you.

CHAPTER 21: PAID TRAFFIC

Before reviewing paid methods, you must understand the different models used when paying for customer.

CPA – COST PER ACTION

You pay people that drive customers to you that take a desired action.

The standard model here is a purchase where you pay through an affiliate program for customers that people send you.

Don't limit this method to affiliate programs, there are many other applications.

You can pay people to send you visitors that sign up for your newsletter or fills out a form. Depending on the market, standard payouts can be as high as $150.

To use CPA, your offer has to convert well or you can lose a ton of money.

CPM – COST PER THOUSAND (IMPRESSIONS)

This is where you pay for banner or text ad placement and no matter how many clicks you get, you pay for how many times your ad is shown.

The key with this kind of advertising is to set it up where those that view your ad or image are given a reason to click on it. Whether you offer something for free or put a decent enough sales message to entice a viewer to take the action you want them to take, you have to put in the effort to get them to do what you want. Animated banners do best to attract clicks.

The key is to have the page they land on converting well.

CPC – COST PER CLICK

This is the standard method of advertising through Google, Yahoo, or MSN. You pay them when one of their visitors clicks on an ad you have placed with them.

PAY PER CLICK ADVERTISING (PPC)

The concept of pay per click advertising is simple. You bid on the keywords you want to rank for and you automatically appear in a location based on the amount of the other bids for the same keyword (the highest bid gets the first spot). It's an easy and automatic way of generating traffic to your website instantly. The key to doing this properly is to do very detailed keyword research. You can find tons of methods of doing this, including through the pay per click search engines you choose.

My secret website for this is www.spyfu.com.

It gives you:

- Average Cost Per Click

- Current Adwords Ads

- Organic Results

- Categories

- Terms Others Buy With Your Main Term

- Related Terms and Concepts

With this you get to spy on your competition and see what is working for them!

Secret website – www.crazyegg.com - Analyzes where clicks are on any page. Tells you what links were clicked on. This gives you a clear look into what customers are doing.

Secret PPC Success Strategies

Success with PPC is guaranteed when you focus on specific elements of your ads.

Keywords: People follow a routine when looking for products:

- Search for a single keyword.
- Search for 2 words.
- Search with brand names.
- Search for long tail terms (3 to 5 words).
- Buy!

What do you think you should focus on with your pay per click strategy?

Long terms!

Use longer and more focused terms. Your conversion will be much higher and you will pay less per click.

Your Ad Copy: There are two specific areas to focus on with your ad copy.

First, you must use specific ads for every term you target. Using that term in your ad will increase click through rates.

Next, the ad itself MUST be attractive to a consumer. People know where paid listings are and normally don't even look at them.

This is a simple fact based on studies of where someone looks on their computer screen while using search engines. **Test your copy, if it isn't working – change it!**

The next piece is your quality score. Having the terms that you are paying for on the landing page you are sending people to will reduce your cost per click.

This must be organic and look natural, once your page becomes spammy, your potential customers will lose interest in you and what you're doing.

Sneaky trick – Do a Google search for your most basic keyword terms. If you sell dog collars, do a search for "dog".

Go through the sites that are listed in the top 5 for this term.

Look for sites that allow advertising or have Google Adwords on their site.

Run a special campaign that posts your ad specifically on this website directly and on the page that ranks well for your keyword.

This will get you a much lower cost per click than if you bid on the term "dog" in Google's main search results.

Secret tip – There are two specific terms that will always attract buyers: Review and Bonus. Review applies to any niche, while bonus applies mostly to Internet marketing specifically.

What to Watch:

- Costs – Set a budget, otherwise you'll end up with a $400 bill in a few days and at least as angry as I was when it happened to me. All pay per click programs come with a budgeting tool, where you can limit the daily expense for your program.

- Click Fraud – The engines do their best to prevent charging you for competitors clicking on your ads. Your competitors will click on your ads to eliminate your daily budget and remove your ad. Once your budget is gone, your ad is gone, too! This moves their ad up and benefits them by costing you money.

- Companies – Depending on how competitive your keywords are, you may want to think about the non-mainstream companies. Google and Yahoo are great, but Exactseek is $4 per month with no click charges. The difference is that they don't send anywhere near as much traffic...

BANNERS AND BUTTONS

I've heard from numerous different experts that someone needs to see your offer 7 times before they even consider it. Banner advertising is the perfect way to take advantage of that. You have a nice looking graphic ad created and pay to have it posted on sites that have traffic that would be interested in what you have to offer.

Your banner should be created with your customer in mind and lure them in to find out more. Curiosity will get you new visitors and customers you may not have ever found. The more they see your ad the more likely they will become curious enough to visit your site for more information.

Your banner ads should be left in place for as long as you can afford to test them. If you get zero results from a banner ad that has gotten 10,000 impressions, then it's time to think about not paying for that anymore. A simple 100 or 1,000 impressions isn't enough to be sure that the right people have seen your ad. The best case scenario with this is to be able to "split test" your banner against a different ad. Simple changes in wording can result in massive differences in click through rates.

Test everything and your results will always be improving.

Finding places to put your banners is not hard at all. Forums are a great place to pay for this type of advertising. Blogs can work extremely well, too. With blogs, be sure that it is content heavy and not filled with promotions of other products. When searching for sites in your niche that you can dominate, look to see if they have advertising and what types they have.

Banner exchange networks exist where you can post banners of other companies on a page and you will get impressions of your own banner based on how many times you show theirs.

Create as many different types of banners as you possibly can.

If you are not a graphics capable person, hire someone to do it for you.

Nothing is worse than an ugly banner ad

Common sizes include:

468 X 60, 120 X 60, 125 X 125, 250 X 250, 600 X 160, and 88 X 31 (measured in pixels).

"Banner Blindness" occurs when you've had the same banner in the same location for two or three months. When people get used to seeing your banners, they don't have the same impact as when they originally see them. You can avoid this situation by having 3 sets of banners created with different color schemes and rotating them every 2 months.

Recently, the term "Media Buy" has become common.

A media buy is simply a large order of paid advertising that can include banner and text ads online, but originated with television and newspaper ads. Any of these types of advertising can be included in a media buy

A media buy is no different from any other paid advertising outside of the fact that you have to spend thousands of dollars for the traffic they'll send.

If you're starting with a large budget and have tested your pages to be sure you'll make money on the traffic you send, media buying provides you with instant traffic without a lot of SEO work.

If you decide you'd like to do a media buy the first thing to consider is where you want to buy the media from.

Do you want to stick to online locations or branch off to television, radio, and newspapers?

Next, you need to take a close look at the media you'll be placing.

Where have you tested it?

All of your media must be tested thoroughly before you do a large scale media buy.

If the media doesn't convert all of these eyeballs into buyers, you can waste thousands of advertising dollars very quickly.

Contact an agency that handles large purchases of advertising and then be prepared to negotiate. Discuss with the company what your plans are for advertising with them and place a small test order to be sure the traffic will convert for your offer.

BLOG AND RSS FEED ADVERTISING

Paying people to review you or your products on their blogs can be an extremely effective way of promoting your business. Find a blog in your niche that gets a ton of visitors and look for an icon that offers paid reviews. Be sure to choose bloggers that have a solid reputation and don't do a lot of reviews for others.

The more objective their review, the better your product looks and the more sales you will make.

Check out Reviewback.com to do free review exchanges.

Every blog comes with an RSS feed, which is a way to distribute blog content to readers and build links pointing to your blog.

Advertising in someone else's RSS feed can be effective with the right feed. You need to be extremely cautious with this one as it has shown in testing to be very hard to track and get pretty dismal results. When picking a feed that you want to advertise in, be sure that you can find out how many users are subscribing to that specific feed. If they don't have numbers for you, don't bother!

Finding RSS feeds to advertise on is as simple as finding blogs in your market that make their money through advertising.

CONTESTS

Having a contest can bring you in tons of qualified visitors. The goal of your contest is to ensure that anybody that may be interested in what you're offering sees the contest and takes part if possible. To do this, do a press release, blog about it, and submit it to these sites:

Be sure you get the most exposure possible for your contest. You want it to pay off, right?

Where you gain your exposure is completely up to you. If you have the time to do it, comment on high traffic blogs in your niche, write articles, pay for the upgrade on PRWeb (a press release distribution site) and get it in front of as many eyeballs as you can.

There are also tons of sites that are specifically built to announce contests of different types. Do a Google search for "contest site" and other variations on that term to find places to announce your contest. The Internet is full of people looking to get stuff for free, so this is the perfect way to take advantage of that.

WEB DIRECTORIES

We are not talking about getting listed in directories for SEO purposes, but traffic. When analyzing directories for traffic you must:

- Find Niche Directories: You need to search for your main keywords and phrases on the search engines to find high traffic sites that may be willing to add your site their directory. Most of these directories will want payment to show your website. Research these sites on Alexa and Google and only pay for the ones that will be worth your money.

- The Almighty Dmoz: Dmoz used to be extremely important because their directory filled Google's. The results in their index still make up the results of hundreds of other directories. The problem with Dmoz is that the editors are finicky. They do what they want, when they want. It can take anywhere from 2 months to 2 years for your sites to be accepted into their index.

- My simple Dmoz recommendation: Submit your websites immediately to Dmoz when you buy the domain name. They won't be looking at it any time soon, anyways. You simply have no way of making Dmoz editors take notice of you and your website. If you pester the editors, they will ignore your site for even longer. Be patient and they will get to it when they can.

- Paid Directories: To gain traffic, the paid directories are the only ones you should worry about. The higher the cost of the directory, the higher traffic it should have. These do not need to be niche specific. Any high traffic directory will work just fine. Two great examples of this are the Yahoo directory and the Business.com directory.

- Format your directory submissions to lure in a customer. Treat it like an ad and they will click on your listing.

BULK TRAFFIC

Sometimes referred to as "guaranteed traffic", this is a way to generate a specific amount of visitors by paying a very small amount of money. You can get 100,000 visitors for as little as $20. Why? Because it almost never results in sales!

This is normally crap traffic that is generated through popunders (your website pops up without warning), robots (software generated visitors), or other sneaky means of making your statistics show that you've gotten traffic.

So what would this type of thing be good for? Ad exchanges where impressions are measured is a great way to use this type of traffic. While not the most honest thing to do, it can get you hundreds of thousands of banner impressions for very little investment. This would also work to get more viewers to a video on a site like YouTube. If a video has been viewed a lot, it gives it more validity in the eyes of other potential customers and can raise the ranking of that video.

CHAPTER 22: OFFLINE TACTICS

Marketing is an absolute necessity for any business that is going to succeed. The problem is that you aren't opening up your mind and thinking about where your customers are. Just because you own a website and do business online, doesn't mean that your customers have to live 1000 miles away from you.

FACE TO FACE NETWORKING

Where are local business people in your area spending their time? This is a question you must ask yourself. Networking with other business owners can not only bring you new business, but help them to give you theirs! Develop relationships with other people that own businesses and you'll literally be amazed with the results you find.

You can network with these business people at your local Chamber of Commerce. Becoming a member of the Chamber is normally inexpensive and provides you with a way to meet reputable people that work in your area. These people already have some success, or they would not be there. Learn from them and teach them and you will both gain from your relationship. This develops a desire for them to help you. Now, watch as the referrals start rolling in.

Organize gatherings through Meetup.com. There are tons of like minded people in your area that have no idea you have the same interest with them. Meetup is a site that is dedicated to bringing you and them together. Being the originator of a group gives you instant expert recognition from other members. Create a simple flyer for your meetings and post them at local grocery stores to get new members and grow your group.

SEMINARS

Seminars are a great place to meet people with common interests and are the premier place to build business relationships. Be yourself and you'll develop a following in no time. When attending a seminar, don't be a wallflower. Stand up and make yourself stand out. There are experts in attendance at any seminar. Reach out to them and offer to help them. Build a friendship and you'll be amazed with the results.

FLYERS & BUSINESS CARDS

Your business card shows your professionalism and gives future clients a way of getting in touch with you for any need you may be able to fill for them. Always keep a stack of a dozen business cards in your pocket, as you never know when a networking opportunity will arise.

Format your card with your picture to guarantee that you are remembered. Also, remember that there are 2 sides to every card. Put a form on the back to allow them to put where they met you and when they want to contact you.

Flyers done on simple colored paper can direct attention to your website. Every grocery store has a bulletin board that people post products for sale and services they offer. Post one for your business! People do honestly read those flyers. Use flyers with tear away phone numbers so someone that is interested in what you do can simply pull it off and call at their convenience.

The next step is to include business cards, flyers, & coupons with any correspondence you have with a customer. You can also add special items:

Branded Pens - Magnetic Business Cards - Key Chains - T-Shirts with your logo, etc…

The more your customers think of you, the more they'll buy from you.

Don't forget the power of a coupon – it gives customers a reason to come back!

THE SIMPLE THINGS

Don't forget the simple things! At the end of your message on your answering machine, mention your business and thank your prospect for calling. Tell them directly to leave a message and refer them to a website with an information capture form.

It is very common to see magnetic signs on the sides of cars. You can get them very cheap on Ebay.

Open up your mind and think of ways you can interact with local customers. If you do it right, you will have more sales.

REFERRALS

Word of mouth is the single best form of advertising. A good testimonial makes people feel comfortable with you and are makes them more likely to pull out their credit card. Specifically ask your customers to refer their friends to you if they need any service or product you offer. If you can, offer them a special discount or small affiliate payment if they refer someone to your site. This gives them motivation to tell their friends and family about how wonderful you are! The best part is that they don't even have to hide an affiliate link – family doesn't care!

The best way to obtain referrals is to make it easy for your customers to get them for you. Utilize tools like Viral Inviter to allow your visitors to refer their friends. Provide affiliate programs as a way for them to get paid for sending people to you.

CHAPTER 23: CLASSIFIEDS

Depending on what you are offering, classified ads can be a great source of traffic.

To generate traffic, your ad must be made to draw in a potential customer. The whole idea behind placing this ad is to get a customer to your website or store, where you can get them to buy your products.

Give good and important details, but don't give too much if the product is for sale somewhere online. It's better to post a link to the website where your product is available and your ad space is unlimited.

You should get into a routine when submitting your ads and come up with as many variations as you can. Craigslist is notorious for catching marketers and removing their ads. Vary up your ads to ensure you get the most out of your efforts.

Include images whenever you can. You can edit your images in any graphics program to include your direct url. **If you are using classifieds for affiliate promotions, be sure to buy a domain and redirect it to your affiliate link.**

CHAPTER 24: EVENT TRAFFIC

Making your marketing into an event can drastically boost the effectiveness of it and can be handled in numerous ways.

Sometimes referred to as a "launch", transforming your marketing into an event gives you the ability to use scarcity as a tool to sell more, interact with your audience, and provide a ton of value at the same time.

The key is to provide value directly related to what you're selling. If you sell information, it should be easy to figure out what to do. Give one of the best pieces of your training away in public over a period of a few days and get your prospects ready to purchase the rest.

When selling physical products, focus on what your products do for those that use it. Ipods provide portable entertainment. Restaurants provide great food and a place for people to spend time together. Toys provide enjoyment for the kids that have them.

Plan out your marketing process for your product launch. It should be at least a few days to give you the opportunity to reach as many of your prospects as you can. Where does your prospect begin and where should they be at the end? Your launch should not be focused on your product or what it is. It must focus on the problem that it solves for those the own it.

Normally, the solution to their problems will be delivered over one to two weeks through video. It can be completed with a webinar or teleseminar.

Webinars or teleseminars can be another way to use events in your marketing. You teach something to your prospects for a set amount of time (normally an hour) that relates to what you sell. Then, at the end of the event, you take the opportunity to make a special offer to those that attended the event.

Scheduling a call or webinar and putting it out to your tribe via social media sites is a great way to get them onto an email list to follow up with them later.

CHAPTER 25: LOCAL SEARCH

With the availability of Internet on every cell phone released in the last few years, small businesses are able to take advantage and get more business from the web with ease.

Local terms like "Cape Coral Dentist" are WAY easier to rank for then the term "dentist" and honestly, you don't want someone in New York finding your local dentist office website anyways.

At http://google.com/local you can easily create a listing for your storefront. The best part is that the listings come up based upon location, not links. You can outrank the big franchise up the road simply by having someone be closer to your location than theirs.

You can also list your business with Bing at https://ssl.bing.com/local/ListingCenter.aspx

Yahoo's local listing service is at http://listings.local.yahoo.com/csubmit/

In a few short minutes, you'll be listed in all 3 of the major search engines based upon your location.

The next step is to optimize your site for search engines based upon your location.

Include your city (if in a very large city, include the suburb or area name instead) in your title tag, blog posts, onsite navigational links, and anywhere else that won't look weird to your visitors.

Then, build as many links as you can with those terms!

CHAPTER 26: SIMPLE IDEAS

Traffic isn't limited to the things you've read about so far, there are tons of other ways to get attention from your market.

Sites like scribd.com allow you to upload pdf files to their site. People will visit sites like this often to gain free knowledge on topics that they are interested in. Scribd™ ranks incredibly well in Google simply optimize your filename, the title, and the description to use keyword terms you'd like to rank for. Always include a link at the end of the file to a product that solves the problem outlined in the file.

How many times have you been looking for a movie, a book, or some other type of digital information and found a torrent site in the rankings? Torrent sites are where you can find almost any movie, song, or training course for free. The problem is that it's illegal to download products you would normally pay for from these sites…

How can you pull in traffic from sites like these? Simply record an audio file giving some ideas or advice that relates to what you sell and recommend that the listener go to your website to find out more about it. This method is extremely hit or miss as most users will be looking for the new movie that hit theaters and not some advice on how to buy the best diapers for their kids, so don't spend much time on it, if any.

What if you had been the person to start Facebook? Can you imagine where you would be now? By paying attention to what is going on with the web right now, you may see the need for something that will help millions of people. Figure out how to get it created and you could soon be able to direct traffic to any site that you want and be earning a ton of money while you do it.

Every now and then, we find ourselves searching for specific products. We find all kinds of crazy results for those searches, but normally, inside of those results are shopping engines. Getting listed in those engines can be great for traffic. They all have their own standards and policies with being listed, so look at sites like Shopping.com or Bizrate.com to see what you'll need to do to be listed in their product directories.

CHAPTER 27: WHAT NOT TO DO

These things either don't work or are not worth the time and effort involved.

Safe lists (there is a catch on these)

Safe lists work for one person and only one person – the owner. Let's think about their approach for a moment. Here is what they tell you to do:

- Supply us with a crap E-Mail Address

- Supply us with a Good E-Mail Address

- Send your Spam to the entire membership (to their crap E-Mail Address)!

If you're lucky, you may get 1 or 2 people to read your message out of thousands. People receive thousands of emails per day from safe lists.

The only value in a Safe list is for the owner. They have your good contact E-Mail address and can contact you whenever they want.

They are literally building an E-Mail list based on the false hope of Safe list mailings creating income for you.

The Point? Don't bother with Safe lists unless you own one!

Free For All Links Pages

FFA link pages are a web page or site where anyone can post ads for free. The problem with these is that hundreds of people post there every day. There are still companies that sell bulk posting to FFA pages. Your results from roughly 2000 FFA Pages will be a lot of spam E-Mail and 1 or 2 visitors. Don't waste your time.

Big Name SEO Companies

The more renowned an SEO Company is, the more expensive they become. Manipulating search engine rankings is a lot easier than you might expect. This book gives you very clear direction on what you should be doing, so follow the book and save your money for some paid advertising.

CHAPTER 28: TRAFFIC BY BUSINESS MODEL

INFORMATION MARKETING

This is easy, do everything.

E-COMMERCE MARKETING

E-Commerce store owners are the ones that approach me most about how they can apply the tactics taught in this book.

What do they write about? What do they talk about?

The simple answer is that you don't talk about the products you sell. You talk about what they provide to those that buy them.

Sell bedding or mattresses? Write about sleep, the differences between different mattress options, and anything else that would interest your prospects.

Sell baby products? Focus on parenting topics.

Sell pet products? Discuss how to increase the quality of life for a pet.

Do you see how this works?

Ecommerce marketers can use any strategy mentioned in this book, all that needs to be done is to focus on the benefits and what their products do for those that use them.

AFFILIATE MARKETING

Affiliate Marketing is a delicate process. Customers don't want to buy from you if they can buy from the original seller. You must also cloak your affiliate links. Here are some specific traffic generation strategies that work well for affiliate marketing.

- Create a review site where you review different new products on the market. Direct traffic to the site and you'll get sales.

- Article Marketing – write about the product itself and submit the article to directories. Be sure to link to an actual web page, without an affiliate link.

- Classified Ads – I recently found someone that makes hundreds of dollars every month by posting affiliate ads to www.usfreeads.com. He posts 10 – 20 ads per day and is making a killing.

- Pay Per Click – Your ads must be different from the others online. Remember that there are tons of other people doing this. Come up with an angle that nobody else is using. Don't pay for top placement, I recommend going for position #3 or #8 as they have given me the best results. Position 3 is just above regular listings and position 8 is the last one on the page. This should save you a bunch of money.

- Blogs – A blog is a great place to set up your home page for affiliate sales. I recommend using a Wordpress blog on your own domain to give you complete freedom. Post reviews and good information about new products and you will definitely get sales.

- RSS feeds – RSS feeds including affiliate links are an outstanding free way to list products in your niche.

- Social Networking – Sites like Facebook can be an excellent opportunity for Affiliates with the correct mindset. Read the previous section for more information.

- E-Mail and E-Zines – Building a list is integral to the success of any affiliate marketer. Sign up for an autoreponder and create a capture page. Give away a free report or Ebook, just for signing up. See the list building chapter for more information on this.

- Add – Ons – Create a product that compliments the product you are selling. Offer this bonus to people that purchase the product through you. This gives them a reason to buy from you.

Do not bother with:

- Web Directories (unless you have a review website or something like that)

- Shopping Sites

AUCTION SITES

Auctions are very well used due to one main thing, **traffic**! You can set up a business on any auction website for little cost and without any other expense.

What works?

- **You Must Buy a Domain Name** before doing any tactics included in this book!

- **Do everything!**

MULTI-LEVEL MARKETING

MLM offers interesting opportunities to people that have the knack for it. You get paid for people entering your downline and selling products your company provides.

Did you know that your MLM website is nearly unable to rank in the search engines, if it is the same as every other member?

The only way to get your website to rank high for your products with a standard MLM site is to link to it like crazy. If you have the most links, you will rank higher than the rest of your competitors.

Create your own website and forward people onto your sign up page from there to gain rankings.

- MLM is often referred to as Network Marketing. There is a reason for this! You must develop relationships and help people succeed if you want to do well with MLM.

- Teleseminars – These work extremely well for MLM. Get a top performer to discuss their success and how they obtained it. Be sure to have them interviewed by someone that knows what they're talking about and it will drive fresh sales.

- Blogs – Setting up a blog for your company is a great way to direct traffic to your sign up page.

- Drive traffic to your blog and website and forward them onto your generic sales page from there. They will get to know you individually and it will help with your conversion rate.

Always check the rules to be sure you're following what the MLM allows. Most of them have strict guidelines when it comes to Internet marketing.

SECTION TWO: ACTION PLAN CHECKLIST

☐ Arrange your keywords in order of priority using the worksheet you get at http://thewebtrafficbook.com.

☐ Distribute your content to corresponding video, article, podcast, blogs, and social networking sites.

☐ Create video, text, and audio content around your customers' questions, needs, and issues.

☐ Inside of your content, place "anchor text" links back to your websites using your chosen keyword terms.

☐ Build a social community by following and actually talking to experts that are already operating in your market to gain attention from their customers.

☐ Test paid traffic methods carefully by using longer keyword terms. Be sure to set budgets so you don't end up losing a ton of money.

☐ Consider using things like tell-a-friend scripts, contests, local marketing, and other ideas that were covered in the book to increase traffic in any way you can.

CHAPTER 30: SELLING THROUGH WORDS.

SECTION THREE: FINAL STEPS

"I've been told that I'm the "best marketer who attempts to write copy". That told me very clearly that I should not attempt to teach you how to write sales copy."

To fix that issue, I reached out to my favorite copywriter, Vin Montello and he sent me this:

The Secret Copywriting Formula That Generates

More Than $3,281,650.00 In Just 8 Months…

"Yes… This Is My Personal

Step-By-Step Blueprint

To Creating Devastatingly Effective,

Cash Generating Copy Every time...

Dear Reader,

Are you tired?

Tired of trying to market a product or service, but not getting anywhere?

Tired of watching your online dreams turn to dust while others around you are setting the business world on fire?

Hey... I understand.

Getting started online isn't easy...

Sometimes it feels like trying to swim through the oil-choked gulf.

Covered in energy-sapping muck...

Each stroke more agonizing than the last...

"A Bone-Chilling Sea Of Pain... With No Land In Sight..."

That's how it used to be for me. Until I discovered the secret that literally turns words into dollar signs; Sentences into huge piles of cash.

Hi... I'm master copywriter Vin Montello.

When I first tried to make money on the Internet I was lost.

All the bad information out there had me running in circles buying and trying every new "gimmick" that promised to make it all super-simple for me.

I grew sick and tired of all the deception. Much like I'm sure you've felt on your trek to financial independence.

Then one day I stumbled upon an ancient book at my local library...

A book on writing that would change my life.

Sure... I'd been a professional writer for nearly 20 years, scribing and producing television shows for the biggest networks and studios. But this kind of writing... man, oh man, this was something I never knew existed...

The kind of writing that had purpose and meaning.

The kind of writing that could make or break any business - new or well established.

It made my heart quicken, my mind race a million miles an hour...

I wanted to write like **that**!

So I studied that book inside and out... Lived with it for months...

I treated that old tome like it was written by god himself, and personally handed to me. I kept it in my car when I took trips... I took it out while eating at restaurants... It even replaced my favorite television shows as entertainment.

This book changed my life in the same way it's going to change yours.

For you see...

This book was all about copywriting...

But more than that it was **_the_** book on writing white-hot direct response copy.

A specific type of writing proven to...

- *Grab the reader's attention and hold it all the way till they get to the "buy now" button, the 800 number or the order coupon...*

- *Tell stories in a way that truly involves the reader. It's well known that facts tell but stories sell... Well, after reading this book your words will sell faster than curtains in a sub-division of glass houses...*

- *Create an on-going relationship with your readers that helps you sell to them not once... but over and over again.*

Don't take my word for it. Here's what legendary marketer and copywriter Jay Abraham had to say about this amazing book.

> *"It showed me exactly what 'salesmanship in print' is all about and moreover, I learned how to actually write the kinds of sales letters that produce astonishing results for my clients... "*
>
> Jay Abraham
>
> Living Legend

And Jay knows what he's talking about.

After all he's been the wizard behind the curtain at some of the biggest marketing campaigns of the last half century.

In just a second I'll reveal the name of that magical book Jay is so jazzed about... The book that changed my life and will soon change yours...

But first I want to talk a bit more about you.

Do you hate starting a marketing campaign

with an empty page? Hate having to begin from scratch with no direction?

Now you don't have to!

Because I created a simple copywriting template based on hundreds of hours of studying that magical book.

A template that ensures you're never left to "go it alone" when you write copy for your products.

"And Now... For The First Time... I'm Making This Magical Template Available For A Crazy-Low Price..."

Here's what you get when you sign up right now...

The Crazy-Effective Super-Simple Copywriting Template: The same template I use as the basis for every multimillion dollar campaign I helm.

I'm not kidding when I say this template is responsible for more than $3,400,000.00 in sales in the last 8 months alone. While its effective worth is in the millions, its real-world street value is more than $1,000.00.

And it's a bargain at that price.

But wait... there's more!

***FREE BONUS 1 ***

The Hold-Your-Hand Breakdown That Explains It All: Here is where I take you by the hand and walk you through the template. This guarantees you're never left alone wondering what to do next.

Having an expert explain it all to you is like having your own personal Sherpa walking you up the money mountain. This expert breakdown would normally cost $~~500.00~~. But you're getting it FREE!

***FREE BONUS 2 ***

The Online Letter Layout: When putting a letter online, getting the layout just right can be a killer. Well... with my template system you get the optimum sales page layout included... FREE! This alone can save you more than $~~1,000.00~~.

"So How Much Is This Going To Cost Me, Vin?"

Elsewhere you would expect to pay thousands for something similar to this template system.

Heck, you could pay thousands for just one sales letter!

And I don't mean from a guru or master copywriter. From them you'd be spending five figures plus. I'm talking about all the other copywriters.

You could hire a relative beginner to write your sales letter for you and expect to pay almost $3,000.00. That's for just 1 amateur-level sales letter.

With my **Copywriting Template System** you get an unlimited supply of killer sales letters for as many products as you have now... and will ever have in the future.

In fact… you are limited only by your imagination…

And you won't pay $3,000.00 for it.

I personally know a copywriter who charges $1,900.00 for a system similar to (but not as complete as) my Super-Simple, Crazy-Effective Template System.

That's nearly two grand!

Still I won't charge you $1, 900.00...

Heck… you could take off a zero!

That's $190.00 for this template, plus the free bonuses… truly a steal.

But I'm not done lowering the price.

So… take off another zero…

That's $19.00 for the most effective sales letter template system anywhere!

But wait… something unbelievable is about to happen…

Remember… you get the CopywritingTemplate (Value: $1,000.00), The Bonus Hold Your Hand Breakdown (Value: $500.00), and The Ideal Online Layout bonus (Saves You At Least $1,000.00) for just $19.

That's a $2,500.00 value all for the price of lunch.

"Hold The Phone... Stop The Presses...

And Any Other Phrase That Will Let You Know

Something Big Is About To Be Dropped..."

Because I want to get this template into as many hands as possible I've decided to do something totally nuts! In fact all the other copywriters I know think I'm crazy for doing this...

But... if you act right now you get the entire package for $00.00!

That's right... FREE!

But you have to act right now, because this amazing **FREE GIVEAWAY** is only for the first 100 who sign up.

After that, the price goes back up to $19.00.

So order right now by clicking below.

Sincerely,

Vin Montello

PS – I almost forgot. Earlier I promised to reveal the name of the magical book that I based my template on. The book I've effectively based my entire copywriting career on...

It's called The Robert Collier Letter Book. It came out in 1937 and it's pure dynamite. Even though you're getting the template system that's based on this book, I recommend you get the book for extra reading. Hunt for it online...

You won't be sorry.

Okay... I'm pretty sure it's obvious to all of you by now that the template I promised is actually the chapter itself.

I thought it would be fun to make the chapter the template, and the template...

"A Mock Sales Letter That Sells The Template…"

Confused?

You shouldn't be. Because if you go back you'll see this chapter/letter follows a simple formula.

1. Get Attention With An Ultra-Specific Headline Package: An eye-catching "secret" concept along with an exact number (not a rounded off number) achieve this. It's also bolstered by the sub-head below it, where the reader is big results in an easy to follow system.

2. Throw Reader A Little Off Balance With A Greeting: The "Dear Friend" part of a sales letter works to make the letter look more like a personal letter instead of an advertisement. But... stay away from the word "friend" if you can. Something more specific to your niche would be better. Dear Marketer... Dear New Marketer... Dear Frustrated Marketer. I like the third example. It's a good pattern to follow. "Adjective + Title..." Dear Desperate Dieter... Dear Angry Mom... etc.

3. Introduce The Problem, Then Make The Problem Bigger: I refer to it as opening a wound, then salting the wound. It's easy. Just mention the problem, then 3 "dimensionalize" it so the reader feels it. Then just as the reader begins to feel it, make him feel it even worse.

First, I bring the pain by mentioning how hard it is to start in this business. Then I amplify the pain by talking about the reader feeling lied to and all alone. That's how you salt the wound.

4. Latch Onto A News Story: It's good to sometimes tie your writing into something in the news. Here I hooked up with the gulf oil spill. Latching onto this type of story will help you ride a wave of publicity, which is like getting free air time. But be careful. Marketing that is attached to a news story will lose its "evergreen" appeal. Put simply, these ads often need rewriting to remain current.

5. Introduce Yourself To The Reader: You can't expect anyone to give you their money until you first introduce yourself. It's often as simple as, "Hi… I'm Vin Montello."

Next… after the introduction you must relate to them by explaining that you know what they're going through. This works to make the reader feel like he/she has company in their despair. And misery loves company.

But it also does more than that. It lets the reader know if you're just like them, and you could do it, then maybe they could do it too.

6. Tell Your Story: I did this in the letter with my story of having trouble in my business until I discovered the Robert Collier Letter Book. I also bring in a little intrigue with my choice of words, and by cliffhanging the reveal of the name of the book.

7. Show Something Unique: I first start by showing how I'm unique, by talking about my past writing television. Then I later show how direct response copy is unique from other writing. And finally I show my product is unique in that it's the basis of all the sales letters I write... and those letters generate millions.

8. Prove All Your Claims: Statistics… endorsements… and customer testimonials are all great ways to prove what you claim. Proving your claims is very important, especially in today's jaded online climate.

In this case I used "borrowed proof." I did this to show a more creative way to get proof. If you have a new product and no proof or in this case, no celebrity endorsements, you can borrow it.

I don't know Jay Abraham personally. I could never expect him to endorse my template. But I know he feels strongly about the book from which the template grew. Therefore I was able to find a quote he made about that book.

Warning: When writing a real letter it's important to track down the endorser and ask permission to "borrow" his quote. Most times they'll let you, but be honest with them.

9. Lay Out Some Benefits And Officially Introduce The Product: It's pretty much self-explanatory. Introduce the benefits of your product in the form of bullets… or as entire paragraphs in the body of the copy.

For those who don't know, a "benefit" is the answer to the question, "What does that feature mean to me?" Feature: "It cushions your pistons." Benefit: "No more tapping and pinging. Your car's engine lasts longer... it saves you money."

10. Guarantee Your Product: Marketing tests show the longer you make the guarantee period and the less restrictions you put on that guarantee, the more people will buy it and less of them will ask for a refund.

It's simple, really. You put few or no restrictions on the return and more people figure well... I could always return it if it sucks. Then you make the period of time in which they can return, long enough (like 6 months or a year)... and it stops them from immediately returning a product.

They figure "well... I've got plenty of time." And the more time they have without returning it... the more chance you have that they'll forget all about it and never return it.

This of course is different in all cases. I'm speaking in generalities. Your mileage may vary, so find the sweet spot for your product.

11. Build Tremendous Value: Before revealing the price of your product, frame the equation in the readers' minds. Justify a higher price for them, so yours will look like that much more of a deal.

If your product is $100, compare it to much more expensive things first. Compare apples to oranges... or **your** apples to much more expensive and inferior apples.

12. Inject Urgency Into The Equation: People love buying stuff today if they think it won't be here tomorrow. Or if the product will be much more expensive by tomorrow. So... give them a reason to fear that. Limit the number sold... or how many sold at this low introductory price.

And if you threaten to raise the price, REALLY RAISE IT. If you don't you'll begin to lose credibility with your market. Many marketers never do this and wonder why their business dwindles.

You can always creatively word your letters to get the maximum sales at the lower price, before the proposed raise. For instance, instead of saying the price is only good for the first 100, say "for a very small amount." Instead of saying "price will be raised in 24 hours" you can say "will never be this low again."

13. Call To Action: The most overlooked part of most advertising is the call to action. Most television commercials never even think of calling you to action. The call to action is plain and simply asking your reader for the sale. It may seem unimportant but studies show that simply asking the reader to buy from you will increase sales.

Actually... TELLING them to buy is far better than even asking. In the above letter I do this with a simple "So order right now by clicking below."

14. Give Em A Reminder: This is most easily done with a PS (Or two or three). Because the PS is the second most read part of a sales letter (second only to the headline) this can be a killer area to captures your readers' attention.

When writing a PS, use it to reinforce the headline, or as I did in the mock letter, use it to reveal something you promised to reveal earlier. Often this can be the payoff to the cliffhanger.

15. Use A Little Psychology: The cliffhanger scenario I use in the mock letter is a psychological device. I build up the secret book, then promise to tell you about it later. This often keeps the reader on edge, reading carefully until the answer is revealed. If you can keep this juggling act going long enough to get through the call to action, you can often enjoy a nice boost in sales.

16. The Online Letter Layout: And finally... I promised you the optimal online letter layout. This is the layout you can use as a starting point for all your letters.

Page (Table) Width: Between 650 and 800 pixels...

Padding (white space in the margins) 26 – 32 pixels...

Johnson Box Width: Approximately 70% of the width of the page...

Headline Size: Between 22 and 32 points (Sans serif font)...

Body Font Size: Between 12 and 14 points (Sans serif font)...

One last note: When adding photos or graphics to your page, make them unobtrusive and keeping with the flow of the copy. And… always caption photos or graphics in a smaller font size.

Well… there you have it. My quick-take sales letter template.

Vin Montello is a direct response copywriter known for some of the biggest Clickbank product launches. Vin and Vin's students usually dominate the top 10.

It's this reputation that earned him the nickname, "The Millionaire Maker."

To read more from Vin visit his marketing blog at www.marketingclambake.com or his home page www.montellomarketing.com.

CHAPTER 31: TESTING

I came to the realization while writing this book that I could easily teach you about anything related to Internet marketing, yet also realized that I can't teach some of the topics as well as some of my friends.

I could have written a page or two about testing, but why do that when I can get the guy is best at it?

A SPLIT TESTING PRIMER

By David Bullock

DavidBullock.com

Traffic. Traffic. Traffic.

The first thing that we hear about when we're establishing a business these days is getting traffic online. And yes, traffic is very important. After your website starts getting the traffic that you want, what happens next?

The fact is you can have tons of traffic coming to your website and still not make a sale, get one opt-in or create any leads. When traffic comes to your website, you want those visitors to do something. That "something," that action is called your most wanted response. Once you really know what you want them to do then you have a goal. Every time they do the desired action, you win. Every time they don't, you lose. This is critical if you are using PPC (pay per click) to drive traffic to your website. Every click costs you money and if that click does not result in the traffic taking the action you want then you are losing money and wasting time.

From here on out, the act of getting that visitor to perform that desired action will be referred to as "conversion."

Again, conversion is another name for the visitor coming to your website and taking the action that you want them to take. Nothing more, nothing less. Conversion is a yes or no metric. Either they do what you want them to do or not.

For example:

> They give you their name and email address – Yes or No
> They purchase your product – Yes or No
> The fill out a form and submit it – Yes or No

You see, with conversion either they take that action that you want or they don't. Your job as the website owner is to make the road to taking the desired action smooth and easy. A lot of factors play into this:

> Readability – How easy is it to read and understand your webpage?
> Color – Are you using the right colors?
> Call to Action – Are your instructions clear in regards to what you want the person to do?
> Source of the Traffic – Where did the traffic that is seeing your page come from?

All these are easy to change and therefore easy to test.

TRACKING AND TESTING

For some reason, people often have a hard time with testing their websites and landing pages. Testing really is silently asking your visitors a few simple questions.

> Question 1: Do you like this? Or do you like that?
> Question 2: Do you like it better if I say it this way? Or do you like it better if I say it that way?
> Question 3: Do you like the way this looks? Or do you like it better if I present my page to you this way?

That's it. Testing is really about asking questions to your visitor and letting them make a decision in the moment. This is what I call a forced survey. Why a "forced survey?"

When you do a standard survey, people know that they are being asked a question. When folks know they are being asked a question for the sake of a survey, many times they change their answers to accommodate the person asking the question. In the case of a "forced survey" you just present the situation to the visitor and let them respond. Either they like it, or they don't. Either they move forward toward your most wanted response and take the desired action, or they don't. It is that simple. Yes or no. Either they like what they see or what you are saying, or they don't.

A forced survey like this is commonly called split testing. That is when you show some of your visitors one version of your webpage or landing page and you show some of your visitors another version of your landing page or website.

Split testing can be as simple as changing the:

- Headline
- Opening Paragraph
- Color of the Background
- Font
- Use of Video
- Use of Audio

Anything that is on the page that the visitor sees is something that can be split tested.

So why do you want to split test your pages? Good question...

Just like when you were in school, testing makes you better. Testing allows you to get to know what your visitors like and don't like. Split testing allows you to better know:

- How to present your product or service
- What pictures they like
- What words they like to hear (or read) when being presented your product or service
- What visuals they like to see as you present your product or service
- What type of benefits they like to hear
- What features they what to know about in relation to your product or service

Knowing these answers will let you fine-tune your site, and you can sell more product or services to the people who are already coming to your website.

Testing can get ultra complicated if you let it. Really, though, it is just getting to know your visitors better and finding out how to best communicate your message to them.

There are plenty of tools that allow you to split test webpages.

One that is free and simple to use is Google Web Optimizer - http://www.google.com/intl/en/websiteoptimizer/tutorials.html.

This video series shows you how to set up a test in about 5 minutes.

How do you know when the test is complete? This is handled by something called Statistical Confidence and Validity. This long word set - Statistical Confidence and Validity – means I did this test enough times to know that it was not a change occurrence and I am pretty sure that what happened during my test will continue into the future as long as I don't change the traffic source. Statistical Confidence and Validity relies on the number of times the page was seen and the desired action was taken in relation to how many times the visitors saw the other page and took the desired action when they saw that page. It is as simple as that. There is some interesting math that goes on in the background. But we don't have to concern ourselves with that here.

Another way to check the validity of your results is to try this tool at the website

LowerYourBidPrice.com: http://loweryourbidprice.com/splittest/.

You'll see that the tool asks for the "Number of Clicks." This is where you enter the number of sales or leads that you have gotten from your landing page. Then, enter the number of people who have seen your landing page.

Do this for version one and for version two.

The math will be done in the background and the program will tell you how confident you can be of your future results for the test that you are running.

Go ahead and play with the tool:

> Enter 100 as the number of impressions (how many times the page was seen) for both Ad1 and Ad2.

> Enter 4 for Ad1 number of clicks. Enter 7 for Ad2.

> You should see a message that reads: **Confidence in the long term outcome of your ads can not yet be**

established. You should let your test run some more to gather more data.

Now enter 12 for Ad2. You should see a message that reads: **Ad 2 has a higher CTR than Ad 1. You can be 95% confident that this result is real, and not due to randomness.**

Notice that Statistical Confidence and Validity is based on the difference in the number of actions taken by the visitors. The larger the spread in the number of actions, the more confidence you can put in the winning ad continuing to win.

So how do you get big differences in response to an ad? The simple is answer is to test big variations for version 1 to version 2.

If you are testing headlines, don't change one word in the headline. Change out the entire headline and the message on the headline.

For example:

Headline 1: How To Train Your Dog To Play Fetch.

Headline 2: Seven Easy Steps To Training Your Dog To Play Catch And Return Games

Big variations in testing should give you some pretty conclusive results.

Split testing might seem like a daunting task; however, it is a skill that is well worth the effort to learn. Follow the steps above and you'll find that split testing can be easily performed and will yield valuable information for converting your traffic to sales.

Same idea said two completely different ways. One of these will work better in the marketplace.

If don't know which one. I have a suspicion but until I take them to the marketplace I don't know.

This brings up a very important point. You can guess and speculate all day long. But until you put the ad, webpage or landing page into the market and let real people see it and respond to the advertisement, you are only guessing and speculating. The true test occurs in the market with real people voting with clicks ands and dollars.

Forget about outcomes and what you think should work and let the market tell you what they like and are willing to respond to.

One very important point to remember: The key to split testing is to only test one thing at a time.

If you test more than one thing at a time you will not be able to keep track of what made the different in your split test.

Don't make this harder than it needs to be. Test (try) something. See if it works and does better than what you had better. If so, keep it. If not try something else. That is all split testing is. Try this then try that.

Finally. You are probably asking yourself so what do can I test? Here's a list to get you

started…

Headlines

Opening Paragraph

Greeting : Dear Friend, Dog Owner, etc

Size of headline

Color Of Headline

Offer

Submit Button Color

Submit Button Text

Guarantee

Closing

Call to action

Images

Video

Audio

Color of the background

The Header Banner

Position of Images on Page

Happy Testing!!!

CHAPTER 32: KEEPING YOUR CUSTOMERS

Once you acquire a customer, it's much easier to keep them than it is to find new ones.

Customer Service is the main thing to focus on to have your customers screaming praise about you and your company.

Personally, I respond to most support requests within an hour (unless I'm asleep, of course).

Think about it like this: You have an issue with a product you've ordered. You're immediately frustrated and upset. You contact the seller and ask for help. Then, you wait for 2 days and the anger slowly builds to a point of near boiling. When you're just about to lose your mind, you finally hear back from support that they'll get back to you soon with a solution for your issue…

It sucks.

You're angry.

You finally get your solution 4 days later and are so irritated, that you request a refund (and wait 4 more days for it).

This is also a great way to create a mortal enemy out of a potentially happy customer, which can lead to a mess on social media sites and their gripes outranking your sales site for the name of your company.

Another mistake that seems to be extremely common is to use an email address for your support. Email gets dropped constantly and lost in cyberspace. Plus, it's very hard to track responses via email. Install a support desk! It gives you the ability to track issues your customers are having and helps you see things you can improve in your sales processes. Plus, it makes you appear more professional.

I have my phone, my iPad™, and every computer I use set to automatically log into my support desk, so I can always help a frustrated customer. Turn the negative situation into a positive opinion of you by communicating with your customers as quickly as possible when they have issues.

Sales are a great way to bring in extra income when you have emergencies or just need a cash boost. It's also a great way to reward those that have purchased from you previously.

Get a toll free number from a site like ringcentral.com to give customers instant access to assistance. I have my number open during business hours and it automatically forwards to my cell phone when I'm out and about. I'm able to answer questions and solve most problems instantly for those that call me.

While I put my toll free number on all my sites, I'm very specific about the fact that I'm busy and can't sit on the phone for an hour to give free advice (I charge a lot to spend an hour on the phone and need to maintain a certain level of exclusivity for those that pay those fees). It's mandatory to let your customers know that you're available to help. It's also a delicate line between helping out a customer and letting them waste time you need to apply elsewhere in your business.

Interacting with your people via social media is another way to increase their awareness of you and your company. I use Hootsuite.com to manage my social media accounts and interact with those that talk to me. I also gab quite a bit with marketing buddies. It lets people know that "I'm somebody" in my market.

Analytics are an important aspect of business on the web (in addition to testing as much as possible). By looking through statistics, you can see which page a visitor leaves from, links they click, and if they purchase from you.

Google's analytics program is completely free and easy to implement (http://www.google.com/analytics/).

Pay attention to pages where customers leave and come up with ways to improve the visitor experience on those pages where people leave your site most.

CHAPTER 33: OUTSOURCING

DANGER!

Seriously.

Outsourcing traffic is something that I've tested like crazy. Any company I've used in the past has always gotten something wrong. The links they build don't get found!

I don't care if you build me 2,000 links in a month for $10 (and it's usually a lot more than that) if search engines are only going to find 5 of them.

Even more important: Most people have no clue about how search engines work, they just know that they need links to their websites. So, they seek out services that are subpar and have no idea that they aren't getting any measurable value. They'll get pretty reports delivered every month that shows them all of these links that Google is never going to find and they're happy. It's appalling.

You, after reading this book, are far more prepared and should consider outsourcing link building and other traffic generation tactics the moment you can afford it.

Big SEO companies are a rip off. Link building services usually stink.

To get around it, you should hire someone and be sure they're trained the correct way to market your business.

First, send them a copy of this book. At least then you'll know they have basic traffic generation knowledge.

Then, be sure they're using my Traffic Magnet software to save time (and cost you less money for their work).

You can get it a trial at: http://trafficmagnetstrategy.com

They'll be ready to rock after watching the videos and submitting a few pieces of content with the software.

CHAPTER 34: YOUR STRATEGY

With all of the information presented in this book, you're probably overwhelmed.

The first thing you should do is register now at http://thewebtrafficbook.com to get worksheets, a mind map, and a special video for free as a special bonus only for owners of this book.

If you're completely new to this, pick the pieces out of this book that appear to be easiest for you to implement. Do those first. Then, move onto the more difficult ones and take your time. Always be adding new tactics to increase your results and market share.

I have been able to make this all work while facing some of the most difficult health issues imaginable, you can definitely make this work for you, too.

The secret Is to do something. Anything. Always be moving forward towards your goals and never sit still and wait for it to happen. Nothing will happen unless you do whatever it takes to make it happen.